De Smith's Judicial Review

First Supplement to the
7th Edition

SWEET & MAXWELL   THOMSON REUTERS

First edition	1959
Second impression	1960
Third impression	1961
Second edition	1968
Third edition	1973
Fourth edition	1980
Second impression	1986
Third impresion	1987
Fifth edition	1995
Supplement to the fifth edition	1998
Sixth edition	2007
Supplement to the sixth edition	2009
Seventh edition	2013
Supplement to the seventh edition	2014

Published in 2013 by Thomson Reuters (Professional) UK Limited trading as
Sweet & Maxwell, Friars House, 160 Blackfriars Road, London, SE1 8EZ
(Registered in England & Wales, Company No 1679046.
Registered Office and address for service: Aldgate House, 33 Aldgate High
Street, London EC3N 1DL)

For further information on our products and services, visit
www.sweetandmaxwell.co.uk

Typeset by LBJ Typesetting Ltd
Printed and bound in the UK by CPI Group (UK) Ltd, Croydon, CR0 4YY.

No natural forests were destroyed to make this product; only farmed
timber was used and re-planted.
A CIP catalogue record of this book is available for the British Library.

ISBN: 9780414036673

Thomson Reuters and the Thomson Reuters logo are trademarks of
Thomson Reuters.

Sweet & Maxwell ® is a registered trademark of Thomson Reuters
(Professional) UK Limited.

Crown copyright material is reproduced with the permission of the
Controller of HMSO and the Queen's Printer for Scotland.

DE SMITH'S JUDICIAL REVIEW

FIRST SUPPLEMENT TO THE SEVENTH EDITION

EDITORS

Professor Andrew Le Sueur
Professor of Constitutional Justice, University of Essex
Barrister, Brick Court Chambers

Catherine Donnelly
Associate Professor and Fellow, Trinity College, Dublin
Barrister, Blackstone Chambers and Law Library, Dublin

Ivan Hare
Former Fellow of Trinity College Cambridge
Barrister, Blackstone Chambers

ASSISTANT EDITORS

David Stott
Affiliated Lecturer in Public Law,
Department of Land Economy, University of Cambridge

Brady Gordon
Trinity College, Dublin

Jamie Susskind
Barrister

CONSULTANT EDITORS

The Rt Hon The Lord Woolf
Former Lord Chief Justice of England and Wales
Former President and founder of the International Civil and Commercial
Court of Qatar
Former Judge of the Court of Final Appeal, Hong Kong
Mediator and Arbitrator, Blackstone Chambers

Professor Sir Jeffrey Jowell QC
Director of the Bingham Centre for the Rule of Law
Emeritus Professor of Public Law, University College London
Barrister, Blackstone Chambers

London
Sweet & Maxwell
2014

PREFACE

The 7th edition of *de Smith's Judicial Review* was published in 2013. The law was stated as it stood on January 31, 2013 (although some later developments were incorporated at proof stage). This *First Supplement* updates the main work to state the law as at August 1, 2014 (though, as before, some later developments have been included).

As in the main work, we have been selective in the cases that have been included. Generally speaking, they either develop a principle or provide a particularly useful illustration of a principle or practice. Although some unreported cases have been included, we have focused on analysis of judgments that have been reported.

A feature of the main work is the use of comparative material, contributed through the guidance of our distinguished panel of "foreign correspondents". As we explain (at para.1–008), comparative material may be useful in two situations: where the law of another jurisdiction is so similar to that of England and Wales that a case could be of practical value as persuasive authority and, more broadly, an approach adopted in another jurisdiction may cast an interesting light on how the law in England and Wales operates or how it might develop in the future. The practicalities of producing this *First Supplement* did not permit us to update the comparative insights offered by the main work. David Stott drafted Chapters 1–5, 11 and 12, Brady Gordon assisted with Chapters 7–10 and 14 and Jamie Susskind produced first drafts of Chapters 13, 16 and 18.

Editors: Andrew Le Sueur; Catherine Donnelly; Ivan Hare
September 2014

TABLE OF CONTENTS

Supplementary Table of Cases

Supplementary Table of Statutes

Supplementary Table of Statutory Instruments

Supplementary Table of European and International Legislation

Supplementary Table of Civil Procedure Rules

Part I
THE CONTEXT OF JUDICIAL REVIEW

CHAPTER 1

THE NATURE OF JUDICIAL REVIEW

INTRODUCTION

The value and significance of judicial review

[Delete all text in para.1–005, but retain existing n.26, and substitute] 1–005

Notwithstanding these restrictions on access, in December 2012 the Ministry of Justice published a Consultation Paper setting out further proposals for reform in three areas: (i) shortening the three-month time limit for bringing proceedings in certain procurement cases to 30 days and in certain categories of planning decisions to six weeks, bringing them into line with the statutory appeal timetable which applied to those cases; (ii) tightening the procedural rules for granting permission to bring judicial review proceedings by removing the right to an oral renewal where there had already been a prior judicial process involving a hearing on substantially the same issue or where the judge, on written submissions, had determined the case to be "totally without merit"; and (iii) increasing the court fee for an oral renewal hearing where permission had already been refused by a judge on the papers but the claimant asked for the decision to be reconsidered at a hearing.[26] The Government expressed concern that the judicial review process was subject to abuse and was used as a delaying tactic, added to the cost of public services, stifled innovation and frustrated much needed reforms aimed at stimulating growth and promoting economic recovery. It sought to justify its proposals by reference in particular to the significant growth in judicial review applications: 160 applications in 1974, increasing to nearly 4,250 by 2000 and over 11,000 by 2011 (largely attributable to challenges in immigration and asylum matters). The proposals were heavily criticised by academics and practitioners.[26a]

[26a] For a critique of the proposals, see Public Law Project, *Briefing on response to consultation Judicial Review: Proposals for Reform* (January 9, 2013); V. Bondy and M. Sunkin, "Judicial Review Reform: Who is Afraid of Judicial Review? Debunking the Myths of Growth and Abuse", UK Const. L. Blog, January 10, 2013; R. Gordon, "Judicial Review – Storm Clouds Ahead?" [2013] J.R. 1. The new time limits for bringing procurement or planning challenges where the grounds for review arose on or after July 1, 2013 and removal of the right to seek an oral hearing where the case was

assessed by a judge as being without merit on the papers were given effect on July 1, 2013 by an amendment to the Civil Procedure Rules. See Civil Procedure (Amendment No. 4) Rules 2013 (SI 2013/1412). A Planning Fast-Track was also put in place in the Administrative Court in July 2013. The court fee for seeking an oral renewal hearing after the initial judicial review application has been turned down was increased from £60 to £215. Certain proposals were not pursued: where there was a series of linked administrative acts, commencement of time limit for seeking judicial review to be when the first such act was committed; and removal of the right to an oral renewal where there had already been a prior judicial process involving a hearing on substantially the same matter.

[Add new para.1–005A after para.1–005]

1–005A The Ministry of Justice subsequently published consultation papers proposing, inter alia, reforms to reduce the use of legal aid to fund weak judicial reviews and proposals for further reform of judicial review.[26b] The proposals included: (i) the creation of a Specialist Planning Chamber in the Upper Tribunal to hear planning judicial reviews and statutory challenges; (ii) extending leapfrog appeals to the Supreme Court in important cases;[26c] (iii) limits on the ability of local authorities to challenge decisions on nationally significant infrastructure projects (subsequently abandoned); (iv) narrowing of the test for standing where the claimant has little or no interest in the matter (subsequently abandoned); (v) strengthening the court's powers where a procedural flaw would have made no difference to the original outcome; (vi) consideration of mechanisms other than judicial review for enforcing the public sector equality duty under the Equality Act 2010; and (v) revisions to legal aid for judicial review cases, oral permission hearings, Protective Costs Orders, Wasted Costs Orders, interveners' costs and third party funding. A number of these proposals are contained in the Criminal Justice and Courts Bill 2014, which is before Parliament at the time of writing.[26d]

[26b] Ministry of Justice, *Transforming Legal Aid: Delivering a More Credible and Efficient System*, CP14/2013; Ministry of Justice, *Judicial Review: Proposals for Further Reform*, Cm 8703. For a critique of the proposals, see Public Law Project, *Judicial Review: Proposals for Further Reform* (October 2013); V. Bondy and M. Sunkin, "How Many JRs are Too Many? An Evidence Based Response to Judicial Review: Proposals for Further Reform", UK Const. L. Blog (October 26, 2013); Joint Committee on Human Rights, *The Implications for Access to Justice of the Government's Proposals to Reform Judicial Review*, 13th Report of the 2013–2014 Session, HL 74/HC 868; M. Elliott, "Judicial Review Reform – The Report of the Joint Committee on Human Rights", UK Const. L. Blog (May 1, 2014); J. McGarry, "The Importance of an Expansive Test of Standing" [2014] J.R.

60; Bingham Centre for the Rule of Law, *Response to Ministry of Justice Consultation Paper CM 8703: Judicial Review: Proposals for Further Reform* (available at *http://www.biicl.org/files/6618_bingham_centre_response_jr-pffr_cm_8703__2013-11-01.pdf*); M. Fordham, M. Chamberlain, I. Steele and Z. Al-Rikabi, *Streamlining Judicial Review in a Manner Consistent with the Rule of Law* (Bingham Centre Report 2014/01, Bingham Centre for the Rule of Law, BIICL, London, February 2014).

[26c] Three changes to the leapfrog appeal were proposed: (i) allowing a case to leapfrog if it raises issues of national importance, where the result is of particular significance, or where the benefits of earlier consideration by the Supreme Court outweigh the benefits of consideration by the Court of Appeal; (ii) removing the requirement for all parties to consent; and (iii) allowing leapfrog appeals from decisions of the Upper Tribunal, Employment Appeals Tribunal and Special Immigration Appeals Commission.

[26d] The House of Lords Committee stage commenced on July 14, 2014. New rules on when legally aided claimant solicitors will be paid in judicial review claims have already been brought into force under the Civil Legal Aid (Remuneration) (Amendment) (No.3) Regulations 2014 (SI 2014/607), reg.5A, which prevent legal aid payments unless permission is granted by the Administrative Court or no order is made and the Lord Chancellor considers it reasonable to make a payment.

THE CONSTITUTIONAL CONTEXT OF JUDICIAL REVIEW

Justification by constitutional principle

[Add to end of n.65]   1–023

See further, J. Sumption, "The Limits of Law", 27th Sultan Azlan Shah Lecture, November 20, 2013 (available at *http://www.supremecourt.uk/docs/speech-131120.pdf*).

JUSTICIABILITY: THE LIMITS OF JUDICIAL REVIEW

[Add new n.93a after ". . . institutional capacity"]   1–032

[93a] In *Khaira v Shergill* [2014] UKSC 33; [2014] 3 W.L.R. 1, the Supreme Court reviewed the application of the principle of non-justiciability in the context of the interpretation and validity of the trust deeds of Sikh religious charities. Lord Neuberger PSC observed:

"[41] ... the term non-justiciability refers ... to a case where an issue is said to be inherently unsuitable for judicial determination by reason only of its subject matter. Such cases generally fall into one of two categories.

[42] The first category comprises cases where the issue in question is beyond the constitutional competence assigned to the courts under our conception of the separation of powers. Cases in this category are rare, and rightly so, for they may result in a denial of justice which could only exceptionally be justified either at common law or under ECHR art.6. The paradigm cases are the non-justiciability of certain transactions of foreign states and of proceedings in Parliament. The first is based in part on the constitutional limits of the court's competence as against that of the executive in matters directly affecting the United Kingdom's relations with foreign states ... The second is based on the constitutional limits of the court's competence as against that of Parliament ... The distinctive feature of all these cases is that once the forbidden area is identified, the court may not adjudicate on the matters within it, even if it is necessary to do so in order to decide some other issue which is itself unquestionably justiciable. Where the non-justiciable issue inhibits the defence of a claim, this may make it necessary to strike out an otherwise justiciable claim on the ground that it cannot fairly be tried ...

[43] The basis of the second category of non-justiciable cases is quite different. It comprises claims or defences which are based neither on private legal rights or obligations, nor on reviewable matters of public law. Examples include domestic disputes; transactions not intended by the participants to affect their legal relations; and issues of international law which engage no private right of the claimant or reviewable question of public law. Some issues might well be non-justiciable in this sense if the court were asked to decide them in the abstract. But they must nevertheless be resolved if their resolution is necessary in order to decide some other issue which is in itself justiciable. The best-known examples are in the domain of public law. Thus, when the court declines to adjudicate on the international acts of foreign sovereign states or to review the exercise of the Crown's prerogative in the conduct of foreign affairs, it normally refuses on the ground that no legal right of the citizen is engaged whether in public or private law: *R. (Campaign for Nuclear Disarmament) v Prime Minister* [2002] EWHC 2777 (Admin); *R. (Al-Haq) v Secretary of State for Foreign and Commonwealth Affairs* [2009] EWHC 1910 (Admin). . . . But the court does adjudicate on these matters if a justiciable legitimate expectation or a Convention right depends on it: *R. (Abbasi) v Secretary of State for Foreign and Commonwealth Affairs* [2003] UKHRR 76. The same would apply if a private law liability was asserted which depended on such a matter. As Lord Bingham of Cornhill observed in *R. (Gentle) v Prime Minister* [2008] A.C. 1356, para.8, there are 'issues which judicial tribunals have traditionally been very reluctant to entertain because they

recognise their limitations as suitable bodies to resolve them. This is not to say that if the claimants have a legal right the courts cannot decide it'."

Limitations inherent in the courts' constitutional role

[Add to end of n.94]   1–033

In *R. (on the application of Reilly and Wilson) v Secretary of State for Work and Pensions* [2013] UKSC 68; [2014] A.C. 453; [2013] EWCA Civ 66; [2013] 1 W.L.R. 2239, in a successful challenge to the legality of the Jobseeker's Allowance (Employment, Skills and Enterprise Scheme) Regulations 2011, Sir Stanley Burnton stated in the Court of Appeal:

> "I emphasise that this case is not about the social, economic or other merits of the Employment, Skills and Enterprise Scheme. Parliament is entitled to authorise the creation and administration of schemes that . . . are designed to assist the unemployed to obtain employment . . . Parliament is equally entitled to encourage participation . . . by imposing sanctions . . . on those who without good cause refuse to participate in a suitable scheme. The appeal is solely about the lawfulness of the Regulations . . ."

Both the Court of Appeal and the Supreme Court held the regulations to be ultra vires.

[Add to end of n.105]

In *R. (on the application of Reilly and Wilson) v Secretary of State for Work and Pensions* [2013] UKSC 68; [2014] A.C. 453, the Supreme Court upheld the decision of the Court of Appeal that the Jobseeker's Allowance (Employment, Skills and Enterprise Scheme) Regulations 2011 were ultra vires because the Scheme did not have a "prescribed description" as required by s.17A(1) of the Jobseekers Act 1999. Retrospective legislation (the Jobseekers (Back to Work Schemes) Act 2013) to negate the financial effects of that decision was subsequently made the subject of a declaration of incompatibility in *R. (on the application of Reilly (No.2) and Hewstone) v Secretary of State for Work and Pensions* [2014] EWHC 2182 (Admin) (July 4, 2014) as being incompatible with ECHR, art.6.

[Add new n.112a after ". . . democracy"]   1–037

[112a] In *R. (on the application of Nicklinson) v Ministry of Justice* [2014] UKSC 38; [2014] 3 W.L.R. 200 a nine-member Supreme Court engaged in a discussion of these issues in the context of the imposition of criminal liability under s.2 of the Suicide Act 1961 on those who assisted suicide. Lord Neuberger stated:

"[72] . . . even under our constitutional settlement, which acknowledges parliamentary supremacy and has no written constitution, it is, in principle, open to a domestic court to consider whether s.2 infringes art.8. The more difficult question . . . is whether we should do so.

. . .

[76] . . . while I respect and understand the contrary opinion, so well articulated by Lord Sumption and Lord Hughes, I am of the view that, provided that the evidence and the arguments justified such a conclusion, we could properly hold that section 2 infringed article 8. . . . More specifically, where the court has jurisdiction on an issue falling within the margin of appreciation, I think it would be wrong in principle to rule out exercising that jurisdiction if Parliament addresses the issue. . . . such an approach would be an abdication of judicial responsibility. . . . given the potential for rapid changes in moral values and medicine, it seems to me that such an approach may well turn out to be inappropriate in relation to this particular issue."

Having said that, Lord Neuberger concluded that it would not be appropriate to grant a declaration of incompatibility at this time. Lords Sumption, Clarke, Reed and Hughes considered that it would be institutionally inappropriate, or only institutionally appropriate if Parliament refused to address the issue, for a domestic court to consider whether s.2 infringed the ECHR. Lady Hale and Lord Kerr, however, did consider it to be institutionally appropriate at the current time and concluded that s.2 was not Convention compliant. The second reading of Lord Falconer's (private members') Assisted Dying Bill [HL] 2014–2015 took place on July 18, 2014.

Limitations inherent in the courts' institutional capacity

Matters in relation to which the court lacks expertise

1–041 *[Add to para.1–041 after " . . . power to exclude a person from the UK"]*

; "secret" trials in the context of terrorist prosecutions;[131a]

[131a] *Guardian News and Media Ltd v AB*, Court of Appeal (Criminal Division), June 12, 2014; *The Times*, June 18, 2014. On the use of closed material procedures in recent years, see paras 8–009 to 8–014.

THE INCIDENCE AND IMPACT OF JUDICIAL REVIEW

Central government responses to judicial review

1–053 *[Add to end of n.184]*

See also *R. (on the application of Chester) v Secretary of State for Justice* [2013] UKSC 63; [2014] A.C. 271, where the Supreme Court agreed that the blanket ban on convicted prisoners' rights was ECHR incompatible but dismissed the appeals of the particular applicants that their rights had been infringed and declined to make a further declaration of incompatibility. On August 12, 2014, the European Court of Human Rights found the United Kingdom to be in violation of ECHR Protocol 1 art.3 in having primary legislation preventing all prisoners voting in the June 2009 European Parliament elections; the court held that the finding of a violation constituted sufficient just satisfaction for any non-pecuniary damage sustained by the applicants and therefore declined to award compensation and also rejected the applicants' claim for legal costs (*Firth v United Kingdom*, Application no. 47784/09).

[Add to end of para.1–053]

In November 2012, the Voting Eligibility (Prisoners) Bill was drafted to give Members of Parliament three options on which to vote.[184a] In a letter to the chairman of the Joint Committee on the Bill dated February 25, 2014, the Secretary of State for Justice, Chris Grayling MP, gave an assurance that "the matter is under active consideration within Government".

[184a] Option 1 would retain the ban for prisoners jailed for over four years; option 2 would retain the ban for prisoners jailed for over six months; option 3 would retain the current ban with minor amendments.

Local government responses

[Add to end of para.1–058 after ". . . general power of competence"]   1–058

, which allows councils to do anything an individual can do unless specifically prohibited by law.

[Add to end of n.198]

The Localism Act was brought into force earlier than originally planned by the Secretary of State for Communities and Government Minister, Eric Pickles MP, following the decision of the High Court in *R. (on the application of the National Secular Society) v Bideford Town Council* [2012] EWHC 175 (Admin); [2012] 2 All E.R. 1175, where Ouseley J. held that the saying of Christian prayers as part of the formal business at the start of council meetings was ultra vires the Local Government Act 1972 s.111.

ADMINISTRATIVE JUSTICE AND PROPORTIONATE DISPUTE RESOLUTION

Internal complaints systems

1–068   *[Add to end of n.226]*

See, e.g. *R. (on the application of Bhatti) v Bury MBC* [2013] EWHC 3093 (Admin); (2014) 17 C.C.L. Rep. 64 (application to reinstate judicial review proceedings in community care proceedings dismissed. It would not be right to grant permission for the proceedings where there was an adequate alternative remedy and where the proceedings could be used as a mechanism for a challenge to new decisions).

[Add to end of n.228]

This is a general requirement. In certain cases, more strict time limits apply.

1–069   *[Add to end of n.233]*

On the meaning of "civil rights and obligations", see *Ali v Birmingham City Council* [2010] UKSC 8; [2010] 2 A.C. 39 where, unlike the entitlement to benefits in *Tsfayo*, the provision of housing to the homeless under the 1996 Housing Act did not engage a "civil right" within ECHR art.6. The award of services or benefits in kind which was dependent upon a series of evaluative judgments by the provider as to whether the statutory criteria had been satisfied and how the need for it ought to be met did not give rise to "civil rights".

Tribunals

Review and appeal in the new tribunal system

1–098   *[Add to end of para.1–098 after "... or re-make a decision itself.[316]"]*

The Upper Tribunal has no jurisdiction to review its own refusal of permission to appeal.[316a] The approach of the Court of Appeal and Supreme Court to considering appeals on points of law from the First-tier Tribunal is "that judicial restraint should be exercised when the reasons that a tribunal gives for its decision are being examined".[316b]

[316a] *Samuda v Secretary of State for Work and Pensions* [2014] EWCA Civ 1; [2014] 3 All E.R. 201.

[316b] *Jones (by Caldwell) (Respondent) v First Tier Tribunal* [2013] UKSC 19; [2013] 2 A.C. 48 at [25] per Lord Hope.

PUBLIC INQUIRIES AND INQUESTS

Other public inquiries

[Add to end of para.1–102]   1–102

In March 2014, a House of Lords Select Committee reported on post-legislative scrutiny of the Inquiries Act 2005. Noting that no inquiry had been set up under the 2005 Act since 2011, but a number of non-statutory inquiries had been established, the committee recommended: "Ministers have at their disposal on the statute book an Act and Rules which, subject to the reservations we have set out, in our view constitute a good framework for such inquiries. Ministers should be ready to make better use of these powers, and should set up inquiries under the Inquiries Act unless there are overriding reasons of security or sensitivity for doing otherwise."[328a] The Government rejected this recommendation (and several others), arguing that "Ministers should not feel constrained from considering other options which may be better suited to the circumstances".[328b]

[328a] House of Lords Select Committee on the Inquiries Act 2005, *The Inquiries Act 2005: Post-legislative Scrutiny*, HL Paper 143, para.300.

[328b] Ministry of Justice, *Government Response to the Report of the House of Lords Select Committee on the Inquiries Act 2005*, Cm 8903 (June 2014).

[Add to end of para.1–104]   1–104

In *R. (on the application of Litvinenko) v Secretary of State for the Home Department*, the Secretary of State refused the coroner's request to replace an inquest with an inquiry under the Inquiries Act 2005, to permit account to be taken of closed material that the coroner was not permitted to consider. The Divisional Court held that the Secretary of State's refusal was irrational.[332a]

[332a] [2014] EWHC 194 (Admin); [2014] H.R.L.R. 6 (for criticism of the court's approach, see Jason N.E. Varuhas, "Ministerial Refusals to Initiate Public Inquiries: Review or Appeal?" [2014] C.L.J. 238, arguing that the court had erroneously approached its task "as though it was hearing an appeal from the Minister's decision rather than exercising a supervisory jurisdiction").

CATEGORIES OF JUDICIAL REVIEW

Convention rights protected by the HRA

1–117 *[Add new n.357a after ". . . away from purely domestic standards"]*

[357a] But the courts are increasingly asserting the power of common law human rights protection independently of the Human Rights Act 1998 and the ECHR. See *Re Reilly's Application for Judicial Review; Osborn v Parole Board; Booth v Parole Board* [2013] UKSC 61; [2013] 3 W.L.R. 1020 at [57] per Lord Reed: "The importance of the [Human Rights] Act is unquestionable. It does not however supersede the protection of human rights under the common law or statute, or create a discrete body of law based on the judgments of the European Court. Human rights continue to be protected by our domestic law, interpreted and developed in accordance with the Act when appropriate." The Convention was not to be treated "as if it were Moses and the prophets" (at [56]). See also: Lady Hale, "UK Constitutionalism on the March?", Keynote address to the Constitutional and Administrative Bar Association Conference, July 12, 2014, p.2 (available at *http://www.supremecourt.uk/docs/speech-140712.pdf*) (". . . there is emerging a renewed emphasis on the common law and distinctively UK constitutional principles as a source of legal inspiration"); and Lord Neuberger P.S.C., "The Role of Judges in Human Rights Jurisprudence: A Comparison of the Australian and UK Experience", Conference speech given at the Supreme Court of Victoria, Melbourne, August 8, 2014, para.29 (available at *http://www.supremecourt.uk/docs/speech-140808.pdf*) (". . . the Judges have tried to bring the common law back to centre stage. The most dramatic example of this is . . . *Kennedy v Charity Commission* ([2014] UKSC 20; [2014] 2 W.L.R. 808. A journalist wished to see the results of a Charity Commission inquiry into the affairs of a charity . . . and based the claim on article 10 . . . we sent the claim back to the trial judge on the basis that we thought that there was a stronger case based on common law . . .").

CHAPTER 2

CLAIMANTS, INTERESTED PARTIES AND INTERVENERS

CONSTITUTIONAL SIGNIFICANCE OF STANDING RULES

[Add new para.2–002A after para.2–002] 2–002

In 2003, the Ministry of Justice expressed concern[8a] that judicial review is 2–002A sometimes used as a delaying tactic in cases that have little prospect of success. The Ministry of Justice claimed that unmeritorious applications could delay government reforms and the progress of major infrastructure projects intended to stimulate growth and promote economic recovery. The courts' wide approach to standing, it said, "has tipped the balance too far, allowing judicial review to be used to seek publicity or otherwise to hinder the process of proper decision-making".[8b] The Ministry of Justice considered that claimants for judicial review should have a more direct interest in the matter to which the application related, to exclude those who had only a political or theoretical interest, such as campaigning groups. Faced with opposition from many quarters, including the senior judiciary, proposals for a stricter test of standing were abandoned (though proposals for financing judicial review may have an equivalent effect).

[8a] Ministry of Justice, *Judicial Review: Proposals for Further Reform*, Cm 8703 (September 2013), paras 67–90. See further para.1–005 above. For a critique of the proposals, see J. McGarry, "The Importance of an Expansive Test of Standing" [2014] J.R. 60.

[8b] Ministry of Justice, *Judicial Review: Proposals for Further Reform*, Cm 8703, para.79.

IN FAVOUR OF RESTRICTED ACCESS

[Delete all text in n.12 and substitute] 2–004

On recent government proposals to restrict standing for claimants without a direct interest, in particular pressure groups, see para.2–002 above.

IN FAVOUR OF A MORE OPEN APPROACH

2–005 *[Add to end of n.17]*

Time limits in certain procurement and planning cases have been shortened to 30 days and six weeks respectively by an amendment to the Civil Procedure Rules: Civil Procedure (Amendment No. 4) Rules 2013 (SI 2013/1412).

ASSESSING THE CLAIMANT'S INTEREST

The role of campaign and interest groups as claimants

2–042 *[Add new n.132a after ". . . within three months of the impugned decision"]*

[132a] In *R. (on the application of Plantagenet Alliance Ltd) v Secretary of State for Justice* (unreported, August 15, 2013), the claimant was a not-for profit entity comprised of the collateral descendants Richard III (king of England 1483–1485), which was formed in response to the discovery of the king's remains during an archaeological excavation in a local authority carpark. The Alliance was granted permission to apply for judicial review of the Secretary of State's decision to grant an exhumation licence on the ground that he had failed to comply with a duty to consult relevant interests as to how and where the remains should be reburied, either prior to issuing the licence or subsequently. Although the application was made after the three-month time limit, additional time was granted. The Alliance was held to have standing and to have an arguable case. *R. v Secretary of State for the Environment, ex p. Rose Theatre Ltd* [1990] 1 Q.B. 504 was not cited. In *R. (on the application of Plantagenet Alliance Ltd) v Secretary of State for Justice* [2013] EWHC 3164 (Admin); [2014] A.C.D. 26, the court upheld a protective costs order made in respect of the judicial review proceedings brought by the Alliance (which had no assets) on the basis that the proceedings raised matters of general public importance. At the full hearing of the claim for judicial review, it was held that there were no public law grounds to interfere with the Secretary of State's decision and the application was dismissed: *R (on the application of the Plantagenet Alliance Ltd) v Secretary of State for Justice* [2014] EWHC 1662 (QB). The Ministry of Justice estimated its unrecoverable costs at around £90,000. The University of Leicester and Leicester City Council (the second and third defendants) were also unable to recover their costs from the Alliance. This case was used by the government to justify its proposed reforms to protective costs orders contained in the Criminal Justice and Courts Bill 2014.

HUMAN RIGHTS ACT 1998 AND THE VICTIM REQUIREMENT

Strasbourg case law on meaning of "victim"

[Add to end of n.152]   2–054

On determining the governmental status of a body, see *Transpetrol v Slovakia* Application 28502/08 [2011] E.C.H.R 2004. Transpetrol was a joint-stock company which specialised in transporting, storing, buying and selling oil. At the time of the contested judgment of the national Constitutional Court, which the applicant complained had breached its ECHR art.6 right to a fair hearing, the state owned 51 per cent of the shares in the company. The remainder were owned by private parties. The applicant had features of both a governmental and a non-governmental body. The court noted, at [65], that the applicant was a commercial joint-stock company operating exclusively under the private-law regime, governed by the Commercial Code, with no privileges or special rights or rules concerning enforcement of judgments against it; subject to the jurisdiction of the ordinary courts; not participating in the exercise of any government power and, in the past, partly owned by private entities (it had since become entirely state-owned). On the other hand (at [66]), the state had always been a major shareholder and at present was the sole shareholder in the company; on account of its national strategic economic importance it used to be excluded by law from privatisation; it had a "natural monopoly" and an unrivalled market position in the state. However, rather than weighing these elements against each other, the decisive considerations for the determination of the applicant's standing under ECHR art.34 lay in "the assessment of the overall procedural and substantive context of the application and of its underlying facts". The genuine issue behind the proceedings was the ownership of the shares in the applicant company, which primarily concerned the rights and interests of other shareholders rather than those of the company itself. In the circumstances, the interests of the applicant company and the government were the same and the application did not strive to further interests other than those that were concurrent interests of the state. The state had also joined the applicant as an intervener in separate proceedings involving essentially the same issues. The application was declared inadmissible for lack of standing under art.34. The court noted, however, that this was without prejudice to the applicant company's art.34 standing should the relevant circumstances be different. But see *Olympic Delivery Authority v Persons Unknown* [2012] EWHC 1012 (Ch), where, in a claim in private and public nuisance, the ODA sought injunctions to restrain protestors from entering or occupying land that was being developed as part of the Olympic site. The ODA was established by statute under the London Olympic Games and Paralympic Games Act 2006, s.3. In exercising its functions it must obey any directions given by the Secretary of State (Sch.1, para.18(1)(b)) who appointed its

15

members and chairman (Sch.1, para.1(1)). It was undoubtedly a public authority (whether core or hybrid) within HRA s.6. Arnold J., however, considered himself bound to balance the rights of the protestors under ECHR arts 10 and 11 with the ODA's rights to peaceful enjoyment of property under art.1 of Protocol 1 (which he did in favour of the ODA). This aspect of the decision is open to criticism on the basis that the ODA, as a public authority, could not argue Convention rights.

Application of "victim" requirement in the HRA

Not a victim

2–057 *[Add to end of n.160]*

Cf. *Re Northern Ireland Human Rights Commission's Application for Judicial Review* [2012] NIQB 77; [2012] Eq. L.R. 1135, where the Commission brought an application on behalf of unmarried couples in a challenge to the Adoption (Northern Ireland) Order 1987 arts 14–15, which provided that adoption orders could only be made on the application of married couples or individuals who were neither married nor in a civil partnership. The Commission had standing under the Northern Ireland Act 1998 s.71(2B)(c) provided there was or would be one or more victims of the unlawful act (which was established).

[Add to para.2–057 before "In Somerville v Scottish Ministers . . ."]

In *R (on the application of Broadway Care Centre Ltd) v Caerphilly CBC,*[161a] where a local authority decided to terminate a care home's contract, the care home was not a victim in bringing a claim to protect its residents' ECHR art.8 rights. Nor did the responsibilities in respect of closure of care homes give rise to a responsibility of the local authority towards the care home such that the care home would itself be a victim of any breach.

[161a] [2012] EWHC 37 (Admin); (2012) 15 C.C.L. Rep. 82.

STANDING OF "PERSONS AGGRIEVED"

2–064 *[Add to end of n.186]*

Some members of the Supreme Court expressed the caveat that there was, however, also a wide discretion to refuse a remedy even though the applicant had successfully established a breach of European Union law, see R. McCracken, "Standing and Discretion in Environmental Challenges:

Walton, a Curate's Egg" [2014] J.P.L. 304; Baroness Hale of Richmond, "Who Guards the Guardians?" (2014) 3 C.J.I.C.L. 100 at 101–104.

[Add to end of n.187]

In R *(on the application of Cherkley Campaign Ltd) v Mole Valley DC* [2013] EWHC 2582 (Admin); [2014] 1 P. & C.R. 12 in a challenge to the grant of planning permission for the development of a luxury golf course in the Cherkley estate, an area of great landscape value and part of which was also within an area of outstanding natural beauty, proof of participation in the process of objection was said (per Haddon-Cave J.) not to be a *sine qua non* to standing, but merely strong evidence that such persons would ordinarily be regarded as aggrieved. Numerous of the directors of and individual subscribers to Cherkley Campaign Ltd not only lived in the area (and could be said thereby to be "aggrieved") but were also involved in the process of objecting to the proposal through bodies such as the Surrey Branch of the Campaign for the Protection for Rural England. Further, there was nothing unfair or improper about a group of aggrieved individuals forming a limited company to bring a claim. Haddon-Cave J. quashed the decision (reversed on appeal [2014] EWCA Civ 567; [2014] P.T.S.R. D14).

INTERESTED PARTIES AND INTERVENERS

Interveners

[Add to end of n.204] 2–068

See S. Knights, "Interventions in Public Law Proceedings" [2013] J.R. 200.

[Add to end of n.205]

See also S. Shah, T. Poole and M. Blackwell, "Rights, Interveners and the Law Lords" (2014) 34 O.J.L.S. 295 which, inter alia, tests the hypothesis that the HRA led to an increase in third party interventions. For a comparative analysis with the Supreme Court of the United States and the Supreme Court of Canada, see L. Neudorf, "Intervention in the UK Supreme Court" (2013) 2 C.J.I.C.L. 16.

[Add to end of n.209]

See also Baroness Hale of Richmond, "Who Guards the Guardians?" (2014) 3 C.J.I.C.L. 100 at 104: "Once a matter is in court, the more important the subject, the more difficult the issues, the more help we need to try and get the right answer."

[Add to end of para.2–068]

An intervener may seek a protective costs order in its application for permission to be heard and/or file evidence, though costs are within the court's discretion.[211a]

[211a] The Criminal Justice and Courts Bill 2014 cl.67 includes proposals that the applicant and defendant (or any interested party) to judicial review proceedings shall not be required to pay the intervener's costs in connection with the proceedings, although the court may make such an order if it considers there are exceptional circumstances. Further, on an application to the High Court or Court of Appeal by the applicant, defendant or interested party, the court must order the intervener to pay any costs specified in the application which the court considers have been incurred as a result of the intervener's involvement in the proceedings. Again, the court has a discretion in exceptional circumstances. During the Bill's second reading in the House of Lords, Lord Carlile commented: "The inevitable consequence of this is that charitable and not-for-profit organisations will no longer be prepared to provide their expertise to assist the court in cases of wide public importance" (HL Deb, June 30, 2014, col.1604).

Chapter 3

DEFENDANTS AND DECISIONS SUBJECT TO JUDICIAL REVIEW

Scope

[In n.1 delete "3rd edn (2005)" and substitute]   3–001

4th edn (2010)

Range of Public Authorities Subject to Judicial Review

Legislation

[Add to end of n.50]   3–011

R. (on the application of Reilly and Wilson) v Secretary of State for Work and Pensions [2013] UKSC 68; [2014] A.C. 453 (Jobseeker's Allowance (Employment, Skills and Enterprise Scheme) Regulations (SI 2011/917) were ultra vires because the Scheme did not have a "prescribed description" as required by s.17A(1) of the Jobseekers Act 1999).

Jurisdiction, Justiciability and Discretion

Jurisdiction of the Administrative Court

Public functions outside the court's jurisdiction

[Correction to n.77]   3–017

Thorburn should read *Thoburn*.

[Add to end of n.93]   3–019

R. (on the application of Khan) v Secretary of State for Foreign and Commonwealth Affairs [2014] EWCA Civ 24; [2014] 1 W.L.R. 872 (refusal of permission to seek judicial review of the alleged provision of intelligence by GCHQ officers to the United States for use in drone strikes in Pakistan. The claims involved serious criticism of the acts of a foreign state and there were no exceptional circumstances to justify the court sitting in judgment on those acts); *R. (on the application of Sandiford) v Secretary of State for Foreign and Commonwealth Affairs* [2014] UKSC 44; [2014] 1 W.L.R. 2697 (the government's blanket policy of refusing to provide funding for legal representation of British nationals facing criminal proceedings abroad was lawful. There was no necessary implication that a blanket policy was inappropriate, or that there must always be room for exceptions, when a policy was formulated for the exercise of a prerogative and not a statutory power. However, the Secretary of State should review the blanket policy in the light of information that the Indonesian proceedings appeared to raise the most serious issues as to the functioning of the local judicial system). In *Belhaj v Straw* [2013] EWHC 4111 (QB) the High Court struck out claims for damages and declarations of illegality relating to alleged unlawful rendition from Bangkok to Libya by agents of the US in which the defendants had allegedly participated by providing intelligence.

[Add to end of para.3–019]

However, the conduct of foreign states in gross violation of established principles of international law or fundamental human rights can impact upon the legality of actions by the UK government.[93a]

[93a] *Othman v Secretary of State for the Home Department* [2013] EWCA Civ 277 (the defendant, also known as Abu Qatada—a Jordanian national resident in the United Kingdom—could not be deported to Jordan to stand trial on terrorism charges as there was a real risk that evidence previously obtained by torture would be admitted at his trial. He was eventually deported to Jordan on July 7, 2013, after the United Kingdom and Jordanian governments agreed and ratified a treaty satisfying the requirement that evidence obtained through torture would not be used against him).

AMENABILTY TESTS BASED ON THE SOURCE OF POWER

Prerogative powers

Nature of prerogative powers

3–030 *[Add new paragraph after ". . . in accordance with the Fixed-term Parliaments Act 2011"]*

Many exercises of prerogative powers are also regulated by constitutional conventions (rules of political behaviour which are regarded as binding by those to whom they apply) and new conventions continue to emerge to accommodate new or changing political times. Under the royal prerogative, the Prime Minister has power to order the deployment of the armed forces overseas. However, it became a political practice to open up such decisions to Parliamentary debate. In February 2006, Tony Blair sought the approval of the House of Commons before authorising military intervention in Iraq. In September 2013, David Cameron sought the approval of the House of Common before deciding on military intervention in Syria. When the Commons did not vote in favour, Cameron declined to intervene militarily. In 2008 Gordon Brown's government had suggested that Parliament's role should be formalised in a resolution to be passed by the House of Commons, but that proposal was not implemented. In July 2013, the House of Lords Constitution Committee stated that there was now an "existing convention – that, save in exceptional circumstances, the House of Commons is given the opportunity to debate and vote on the deployment of armed forces overseas".[135a]

[135a] House of Lords Constitution Committee, *Constitutional Arrangements for the Use of Armed Force*, Second Report of 2013–2014, HL Paper 46, para.64.

Shift from jurisdiction to justiciability to set limits on court's powers to supervise legality of prerogative powers

[Add new n.143a after ". . . or a refusal to dissolve Parliament"]   3–033

[143a] The prerogative power of dissolution of Parliament prior to a general election has been overtaken by the Fixed Term Parliaments Act 2011: see para.3–030 above.

[Add to para.3–033 after ". . . excluding a person from the UK;[151]"]   3–033

inclusion of a person on the United Nations Security Council's list of persons associated with terrorist organisations and the European Union's sanctions list;[151a]

[151a] *R. (on the application of Youssef) v Secretary of State for Foreign and Commonwealth Affairs* [2013] EWCA Civ 1302; [2014] 2 W.L.R. 1082.

[Add to end of n.153]

In an answer to a Written Question, the Secretary of State for Northern Ireland revealed that the Royal Prerogative of Mercy had been used "in Northern Ireland 365 times between 1979 and 2002, but this total does not include the period between 1987 and 1997 for which records cannot currently be found" and "There are no cases where the RPM has been granted since the current Government came to office in May 2010, and the records indicate that there are no instances where the RPM was granted after 2002" (HC Deb, May 1, 2014, c762W). It was not clear how many of those pardoned were members of paramilitary groups or members of the security services, but the Northern Ireland Office said that the vast majority were not terrorism-related and examples of use "included driving offences, assault, burglary, theft and non-payment of national insurance contributions" (BBC News, "Royal Prerogative of Mercy: Over 350 issued in Northern Ireland", May 2, 2014 (available at *http://www.bbc.co.uk/news/uk-northern-ireland–27260596*)). The NIO also highlighted that the prerogative of mercy had been used much more frequently before the establishment of the Criminal Cases Review Commission in 1997. In December 2013 the wartime code breaker, Alan Turing, was granted a posthumous pardon by the Queen at the request of the Secretary of State for Justice (Chris Grayling MP). Turing had been convicted of an offence of gross indecency in 1952 for engaging in homosexual activity and had been chemically castrated (Ministry of Justice, "Press Release: Royal Pardon for WW2 code-breaker Dr Alan Turing", December 24, 2013 (available at *https://www.gov.uk/government/news/royal-pardon-for-ww2-code-breaker-dr-alan-turing*)).

[Add to end of n.154]

This duty does not extend to the provision of funding for legal representation of British nationals facing criminal proceedings abroad. *R. (on the application of Sandiford) v Secretary of State for Foreign and Commonwealth Affairs* [2014] UKSC 44; [2014] 1 W.L.R. 2697.

Prerogative powers in respect of which the court may not have supervisory jurisdiction

3–034   *[At end of n.161 delete "3rd edn (2005)" and substitute]*

4th edn (2010)

AMENABILITY OF FUNCTIONS RELATING TO PRECONTRACTUAL AND CONTRACTUAL POWERS

Amenability tests for contractual situations

3–057   *[Add to end of n.239]*

R. (on the application of Trafford) v Blackpool BC [2014] EWHC 85; [2014] 2 All E.R. 947 (decision not to renew lease to firm of solicitors who had acted for claimants in personal injuries claims against the council held to be amenable to judicial review). Per H.H. Judge Stephen Davies: "At the very least there is a sufficient public element or connection to render the decision amenable to judicial review on the ground of abuse of power, whether categorised as improper or unauthorised power." See also para.11–072 n.259.

Identifying the "additional public element"

Situations where there was a sufficient "additional public element"

[Add to end of para.3–062]   3–062

Also, where a sub-contractor to run a breakdown recovery service for the police was refused a vetting clearance without reasons.[259a]

[259a] *R. (on the application of A) v Chief Constable of B* [2012] EWHC 2141; [2012] A.C.D. 125.

AMENABILITY AND THE HUMAN RIGHTS ACT

"Functions of a public nature" under the HRA

The YL decision in the House of Lords

[Add to end of n.319]   3–078

A. Williams, "A Fresh Perspective on Hybrid Public Authorities under the Human Rights Act 1998: Private Contractors, Rights-stripping and 'Chameleonic' Horizontal Effect" [2011] P.L. 139.

[Add new paragraph at end of 3–079]   3–079

Section 145 afforded protection to those whose care was arranged under the National Assistance Act 1948 but not those whose care was arranged outside the 1948 Act—for example, those who receive care in a home but pay for it themselves and those who receive care at home by an independent provider. This loophole was closed by s.73 of the Care Act 2014.[324a]

[324a] Section 73 reads:

"Human Rights Act 1998: provision of regulated care or support etc a public function

(1) This section applies where—

    (a) in England, a registered care provider provides care and support to an adult or support to a carer, in the course of providing—

        (i) personal care in a place where the adult receiving the personal care is living when the personal care is provided, or

        (ii) residential accommodation together with nursing or personal care;

    (b) in Wales, a person registered under Part 2 of the Care Standards Act 2000 provides care and support to an adult, or support to a carer, in the course of providing—

        (i) personal care in a place where the adult receiving the personal care is living when the personal care is provided, or

        (ii) residential accommodation together with nursing or personal care;

    (c) in Scotland, a person provides advice, guidance or assistance to an adult or support to a carer, in the course of providing a care service which is registered under section 59 of the Public Services Reform (Scotland) Act 2010 and which consists of the provision of—

        (i) personal care in a place where the adult receiving the personal care is living when the personal care is provided, or

        (ii) residential accommodation together with nursing or personal care;

    (d) in Northern Ireland, a person registered under Part 3 of the Health and Personal Social Services (Quality, Improvement and Regulation) (Northern Ireland) Order 2003 provides advice, guidance or assistance to an adult or services to a carer, in the course of providing—

        (i) personal care in a place where the adult receiving the personal care is living when the personal care is provided, or

        (ii) residential accommodation together with nursing or personal care.

In this section "the care or support" means the care and support, support, advice, guidance, assistance or services provided as mentioned above, and "the provider" means the person who provides the care or support.

(2) The provider is to be taken for the purposes of section 6(3)(b) of the Human Rights Act 1998 (acts of public authorities) to be exercising a function of a public nature in providing the care or support, if the requirements of subsection (3) are met.

(3) The requirements are that—

    (a) the care or support is arranged by an authority listed in column 1 of the Table below, or paid for (directly or indirectly, and in whole or in part) by such an authority, and

(b) the authority arranges or pays for the care or support under a provision listed in the corresponding entry in column 2 of the Table."

Overview of the case law

[Add to end of n.335]   3–080

See also *R. (on the application of Bevan & Clarke LLP) v Neath Port Talbot CBC* [2012] EWHC 236 (Admin); [2012] B.L.G.R. 728 (private sector operators of care homes applied for judicial review of local authority's decision to award a 5.7 per cent increase in the rate to be paid to them. The decision was amenable to judicial review. The mere fact that it concerned the setting of a fee under a contract did not characterise it as a private act. The application failed on other grounds).

TERRITORIAL JURISDICTION AND THE HRA

[Delete text in n.427 from "For UK case law, see: Smith and others v Ministry   3–094
of Defence [2012] EWCA Civ 1365; [2013] 2 W.L.R. 27 ..." and
substitute]

For UK case law, see *Smith v Ministry of Defence* [2013] UKSC 41; [2014] A.C. 52 (in civil claims brought by families of British soldiers killed in Iraq, arguing that they had not been provided with adequate protective equipment, the Supreme Court, following the decision of the Grand Chamber in *Al-Skeini v United Kingdom* (above) held, reversing the decision of the Court of Appeal [2012] EWCA Civ 1365; [2013] 2 W.L.R. 27, that the United Kingdom's jurisdiction under art.1 of the ECHR extended to securing the protection of art.2 to members of the armed forces when serving outside its territory. The statement in *Al-Skeini* that "whenever the state through its agents exercises control and authority over an individual, and thus jurisdiction" stated the circumstances in which the state could be held to exercise jurisdiction extraterritorially. The state was under an obligation under art.1 to secure to the individuals over whom it had such authority and control the rights and freedoms under art.1 of the Convention relevant to their situation. The previous decision of the Supreme Court in *R. (on the application of Smith) v Oxfordshire Assistant Deputy Coroner* [2010] UKSC 29; [2011] 1 A.C. 1 that, unless they were on a UK military base, British troops on active service overseas were not within Convention jurisdiction was not followed). In *R. (on the application of Sandiford) v Secretary of State for Foreign and Commonwealth Affairs* [2014] UKSC 44; [2014] 1 W.L.R. 2697, S, who was facing the death penalty in Indonesia following her conviction for drug trafficking, was not within the jurisdiction of the United

Kingdom for the purposes of ECHR art.1 and so no part of ECHR art.6 could impose an obligation on the United Kingdom to provide funding for legal representation in an application to the Indonesian Supreme Court to re-open her case or an application to the President for clemency in order to avoid execution.

CHAPTER 4

CONCEPTS OF JURISDICTION AND LAWFUL ADMINISTRATION

STATUTORY RESTRICTION OF JUDICIAL REVIEW

[Add to para.4–016 after ". . . or to a provision that conferred exclusive juris- **4–016**
diction on the Investigatory Powers Tribunal.[40]"]

By comparison, a provision that, in given circumstances, conferred jurisdiction over exclusion and naturalisation decisions on the Special Immigration Appeals Commission rather than the High Court, did not enable the Secretary of State to stay existing judicial review proceedings challenging such decisions and transfer them to SIAC. The statutory provisions were too general to confer such a power on the Secretary of State. Specific and express language was expected.[40a]

[40a] See *R. (on the application of Ignaoua) v Secretary of State for the Home Department* [2013] EWCA Civ 1498; [2014] 1 W.L.R. 651, reversing [2013] EWHC 2512 (Admin); [2014] A.C.D. 37 on the interpretation of the Justice and Security Act 2013 s.15, which reads:
   "(1) Subsection (2) applies in relation to any direction about the exclusion of a non-EEA national from the United Kingdom which—
      (a) is made by the Secretary of State wholly or partly on the ground that the exclusion from the United Kingdom of the non-EEA national is conducive to the public good,
      (b) is not subject to a right of appeal, and
      (c) is certified by the Secretary of State as a direction that was made wholly or partly in reliance on information which, in the opinion of the Secretary of State, should not be made public—
         (i) in the interests of national security,
         (ii) in the interests of the relationship between the United Kingdom and another country, or
         (iii) otherwise in the public interest.
   (2) The non-EEA national to whom the direction relates may apply to the Special Immigration Appeals Commission to set aside the direction.
   (3) In determining whether the direction should be set aside, the Commission must apply the principles which would be applied in judicial review proceedings."

The judicial review proceedings were, however, subsequently stayed by the Divisional Court itself and transferred to SIAC: *R. (on the application of Ignaoua) v Secretary of State for the Home Department* [2014] EWHC 1382 (Admin).

Time-limited clauses

4–025 *[Add new n.77a after ". . . in any legal proceedings whatsoever"]*

[77a] New time limits for bringing a judicial review in certain planning cases (six weeks) and in certain procurement cases (30 days) were given effect on July 1, 2013 by an amendment to the Civil Procedure Rules: see Civil Procedure (Amendment No.4) Rules 2013 (SI 2013/1412):

"Amendments to the Civil Procedure Rules 1998
  4. In Part 54—

(a) in rule 54.5—
  (i) before paragraph (1), insert—

'(A1) In this rule—
  'the planning acts' has the same meaning as in section 336 of the Town and Country Planning Act 1990(1);
  'decision governed by the Public Contracts Regulations 2006(2)' means any decision the legality of which is or may be affected by a duty owed to an economic operator by virtue of regulation 47A of those Regulations (and for this purpose it does not matter that the claimant is not an economic operator); and
  'economic operator' has the same meaning as in regulation 4 of the Public Contracts Regulations 2006.';

(ii) in paragraph (2), for 'limit' substitute 'limits'; and
(iii) after paragraph (3), insert—

'(4) Paragraph (1) does not apply in the cases specified in paragraphs (5) and (6).
  (5) Where the application for judicial review relates to a decision made by the Secretary of State or local planning authority under the planning acts, the claim form must be filed not later than six weeks after the grounds to make the claim first arose.
  (6) Where the application for judicial review relates to a decision governed by the Public Contracts Regulations 2006, the claim form must be filed within the time within which an economic operator would have been required by regulation 47D(2) of those Regulations (and disregarding the rest of that regulation) to start any proceedings under those Regulations in respect of that decision.'"

THE ANISMINIC CASE

Criminal proceedings

[Add new n.111a after ". . . subject now to the Criminal Justice Act 2003   **4–038**
Pt 10"]

111a For the position in Scotland, see the Double Jeopardy (Scotland) Act
2011.

Review of courts and tribunals

[Add to end of para.4–040]   **4–040**

The second-tier appeals test places the emphasis on important points of law
or principle or other compelling reasons.127a

127a On the application of the second-tier appeals test, see *PR (Sri Lanka)*
v Secretary of State for the Home Department [2011] EWCA Civ 988; [2012]
1 W.L.R. 73 (the "other compelling reasons" test was to be an exceptional
remedy; "compelling" meant legally compelling, rather than politically or
emotionally though extreme consequences might exceptionally add weight
to the legal arguments); *JD (Congo) v Secretary of State for the Home*
Department [2012] EWCA Civ 327; [2012] 1 W.L.R. 3273 (the fact that an
appellant had succeeded in the First-tier Tribunal (FTT) but failed in the
Upper Tribunal (UT) or that the FTT's decision had been set aside and
remade by the UT could be a relevant factor in applying the "other compelling reason" test; further, approving *PR*, in the absence of a strongly arguable
error of law on the part of the UT, extreme consequences could not of
themselves amount to a free-standing "compelling reason"); *R. (on the appli-*
cation of HS) v Upper Tribunal (Immigration and Asylum Chamber) [2012]
EWHC 3126; [2013] Imm. A.R. 579 (the second-tier appeals criteria
were to be satisfied at the permission stage; it was not sufficient to establish
that they would be satisfied at the substantive hearing; if permission was
granted on that basis, the test was spent and the Court of Appeal had to
apply the established grounds for judicial review in determining whether the
decision of the UT to refuse permission to appeal should be set aside); cf. *A*
v Secretary of State for the Home Department [2013] EWHC 1272 (Admin)
(applicants wrongly treated as non-EU nationals and made subject to depor-
tation orders; multiple failures by the FTT and the UT amounted to a
"compelling reason").

Jurisdiction and Vires Today

Precedent fact

4–052 *[Add to end of para.4–052]*

However, a mistaken but reasonable belief that a person was over 18 did not render detention pending removal from the United Kingdom in breach of the Home Secretary's statutory duty regarding the welfare of children unlawful.[176a]

[176a] *R. (AA (Afghanistan)) v Secretary of State for the Home Department* [2013] UKSC 49; [2013] 1 W.L.R. 2224 (Borders, Citizenship and Immigration Act 2009 s.55, required the Home Secretary to make arrangements for ensuring that her immigration functions were discharged having regard to the need to safeguard and promote the welfare of children; an initial local authority age assessment had concluded that the person was over 19 years of age on which basis the Home Secretary refused an asylum claim and made a detention order; a subsequent local authority age assessment concluded that the person was 17 and the Home Secretary conceded that, had she known this, she would not have made the order).

From "Void and Voidable" to "Lawful and Unlawful"

The situation today

Presumption of validity

4–059 *[Add to end of n.190]*

See also D. Feldman, "Error of Law and Flawed Administrative Acts" [2014] C.L.J. 273, where it is argued that seven principles operate alongside the proposition that all legal flaws make a decision void as a matter of law and "can mitigate its potential to operate in anti-social ways in some circumstances".

Residual categories

4–061 *[Add new n.200a after "The Prevention of Terrorism Act 2005"]*

[200a] Repealed by the Terrorism Prevention and Investigation Measures Act 2011, which replaced "control orders" with "Terrorism Prevention and Investigation Measures" (TPIMs).

Part II
GROUNDS OF JUDICIAL REVIEW

CHAPTER 5

ILLEGALITY

DISCRETIONARY POWER: A BRIEF HISTORY OF JUDICIAL ATTITUDES

Change of approach

[Add to para. 5–018 after ". . . that included a substantial subjective element"] 5–018

The *Padfield* principle also applies to a failure to exercise a power.[44a]

[44a] In *M v Scottish Ministers* [2012] UKSC 58; [2012] 1 W.L.R. 3386 the Mental Health (Care and Treatment) (Scotland) Act 2003 enabled patients compulsorily detained in hospital to apply to a mental health tribunal for a declaration that they were being held in conditions of excessive security. The provisions applied, inter alia, to "qualifying patients" in "qualifying hospitals", to be defined in ministerial regulations. The Act provided that the provisions were to come into force no later than May 1, 2006 but no regulations were ever made. In an application for judicial review, the Scottish Ministers argued a distinction between a statute coming into force and a statute coming into operation and that the failure to make regulations had not defeated the intention of the Scottish Parliament in defining the date when the statute should come into force. The Lord Ordinary refused the petition and the Inner House of the Court of Session refused the petitioner's reclaiming motion. But the Supreme Court allowed the petitioner's appeal—in the judgment of the court, Lord Reed held at [42]–[43], [47]:

> "It has long been a basic principle of administrative law that a discretionary power must not be used to frustrate the object of the Act which conferred it . . . it follows that, although the Ministers had a discretion as to the manner in which they exercised their power to make the necessary regulations, they were under a duty to exercise that power no later than 1 May 2006 . . . although (the relevant sections) are technically in force, they have no more practical effect today than they had . . . when the 2003 Act received the Royal Assent. The Ministers' failure to make the necessary regulations has thus thwarted the intention of the Scottish Parliament . . . The importance of *Padfield's case* [1968] AC 997 was its reassertion that, even where a statute confers a discretionary power, a failure to exercise the power will be unlawful if it is contrary to Parliament's intention.

That intention may be to create legal rights which can only be made effective if the power is exercised . . . It may however be to bring about some other result which is similarly dependent upon the exercise of the power . . . In the present case, the exercise of the power to make regulations by 1 May 2006 was necessary in order to bring (the relevant part) of the 2003 Act into effective operation by that date, as the Scottish Parliament intended. The Ministers were therefore under an obligation to exercise the power by that date."

Cf. R. (on the application of Great Yarmouth Port Co. Ltd) v Marine Management Organisation [2014] EWHC 833 (a discretionary power to make a harbour revision order if certain preconditions were met did not compel the making of such an order once the preconditions were met. There remained a residual discretion to refuse to make an order).

STATUTORY INTERPRETATION

5–020   [Add to para.5–020 after ". . . has also been construed in various contexts.[53]"]

The Supreme Court was called upon to determine the meaning of "stateless" in the British Nationality Act 1981.[53a]

[53a] Al-Jedda v Secretary of State for the Home Department [2013] UKSC 62; [2014] A.C. 253 (under s.40(2) of the British Nationality Act 1981, the Secretary of State may not make an order depriving a person of citizenship if "satisfied that the order would make a person stateless". It was not open to the Secretary of State to argue that the cause of statelessness was a failure on the part of the applicant to apply for restoration of Iraqi nationality rather than the making of the order).

[Add to end of para.5–020]

Where the Secretary of State appointed a trust special administrator to a failing NHS trust pursuant to the statutory regime contained in Ch.5A of the National Health Service Act 2006, the words "action . . . in relation to the trust" meant the trust special administrator could make recommendations only in relation to that specific NHS trust and the Secretary of State accordingly acted unlawfully in accepting recommendations relating to a neighbouring NHS trust.[56a]

[56a] R. (on the application of Lewisham LBC) v Secretary of State for Health; R. (on the application of Save Lewisham Hospital Campaign Ltd) v Secretary of State for Health [2013] EWCA Civ 1409; [2014] 1 W.L.R. 514.

Non-statutory sources of power and the Ram doctrine

[Delete all text in n.86 and substitute]   5–027

See House of Lords Constitution Committee, *The pre-emption of Parliament*, 13th Report of 2012–2013, HL Paper 165. The Committee found no widespread or egregious use of pre-emption but made the following recommendations:

i.   All instances of pre-emption must be governed by certain fundamental constitutional principles, including the rule of law and effective parliamentary scrutiny.

ii. The Treasury plays an important role in policing this area within Government. However, the Treasury's practices carry no constitutional force, and should not be described so as to suggest otherwise. In particular, its practice of authorising certain expenditure once a bill has been given a second reading in the House of Commons is not a constitutional convention and has not been endorsed by Parliament.

iii. As there is no standard procedure at present, the Government must do more to inform Parliament of their pre-emptive activities. Written statements should be made to Parliament in a timely manner, setting out details of each instance of pre-emption and justifying it; and a statement should be made at the end of each session giving an annual summary of pre-emptive activities.

iv. Similarly, a written ministerial statement should be made at the end of each session on the number of ministerial directions issued in the session.

v.   Where pre-emption occurs, the Government must always state clearly the power under which they consider themselves authorised to act.

vi. The principles and practices governing pre-emption should be consolidated into a single, authoritative restatement for inclusion in the Cabinet Manual.

vii. The common law powers of the Crown are restrained by public law and constitutional principle. This should be made clear in all Government publications mentioning these powers.

viii. The so-called "Ram doctrine", which has been invoked to support pre-emption, is misleading and inaccurate, and should no longer be used.

ix. Pre-emption of Parliament should not be undertaken when it would threaten the principle of effective parliamentary scrutiny. The Government's response in October 2013 accepted "that the advice in the Ram opinion is necessarily incomplete because it predates important developments in public law, as well as the Human Rights Act. Nor can it have the force of law. But the Government believes that principle described in the Ram opinion does remain valid. That is, the Crown does have common law powers which may be exercised subject to overarching legal constraints" (see *http://www.parliament.uk/documents/lords-committees/constitution/GovernmentResponse/Government%20response%20-%20report%20on%20pre-emption%20of%20parliament.pdf*).

The discovery of Parliament's intent and use of Hansard

5–032 *[Delete text in n.101 from "At the time of writing . . ." and substitute]*

For Parliament's response to the European Court of Human Right's judgment, see para.1–053 above.

Overarching statutory duties

5–039 *[Add to end of n.120]*

The main question in relation to the PSED is not whether the outcome is justifiable, but whether, in the process leading to the making of the decision, the decision-maker had "due regard" to the relevant considerations. For a summary of the case law on the correct approach, see *R. (on the application of Bracking) v Secretary of State for Work and Pensions* [2013] EWCA Civ 1345; [2014] Eq. L.R. 60 at [25] (McCombe L.J.) and see para.5–072 below.

Interpretation in relation to constitutional principles and constitutional rights

5–040 *[Add to end of n.124]*

In *Re Reilly's Application for Judicial Review; Osborn v Parole Board; Booth v Parole Board* [2013] UKSC 61; [2013] 3 W.L.R. 1020 at [57], Lord Reed stated: "The importance of the [Human Rights] Act is unquestionable. It does not however supersede the protection of human rights under the common law or statute, or create a discrete body of law based on the judgments of the European Court. Human rights continue to be protected by our domestic law, interpreted and developed in accordance with the Act when appropriate." See also para.1–117 above.

5–042 *[Add to end of n.141]*

R. (on the application of the Public Law Project) v Secretary of State for Justice [2014] EWHC 2365 (an amendment by secondary legislation to the Legal Aid, Sentencing and Punishment of Offenders Act 2012 introducing a residence test for eligibility to legal aid was ultra vires. The power to make delegated legislation had to be construed in the context of the statutory policy and aims. The primary objective of the Act was based on funding those with a priority need. The residence test was focussed entirely on reducing cost).

[Add to n.144 before "See also ECHR art.6 . . ."]

But see *Guardian News and Media Ltd v AB*, Court of Appeal (Criminal Division), June 12, 2014; *The Times*, June 18, 2014, where Gross L.J. stated at [2]: "Open justice is both a fundamental principle of the common law and a means of ensuring public confidence in our legal system: exceptions are rare and must be justified on the facts. Any such exceptions must be necessary and proportionate. No more than the minimum departure from open justice will be countenanced." However, open justice must give way to "the yet more fundamental principle that the paramount object of the Court is to *do* justice" (at [5]). This case was "exceptional" and, as a matter of necessity, the *core* (emphasis supplied) of the trial must be heard *in camera*. See also paras 8–009 to 8–014.

MANDATORY AND DIRECTORY DUTIES AND POWERS

[Add to end of n.199]   5–057

R. v Stocker [2013] EWCA Crim 1993; [2014] 1 Cr. App. R. 18 (appeal against rape conviction on the basis that the defendant had been indicted under the wrong Act dismissed even though the Criminal Procedure Rules 2013 stated that the indictment "must" identify the legislation that created the offence. The clear purpose of the relevant rule was to ensure that an accused had sufficient information to know the case he had to meet. The error was a pure technicality that had caused no prejudice. It was not so fundamental as to render the proceedings a nullity and the draftsman would not have intended such an outcome for such a breach); *Aylesbury Vale DC v Call a Cab Ltd* [2013] EWHC 3765 (Admin); [2014] P.T.S.R. 523 (although the Local Government (Miscellaneous Provisions) Act 1976 s.45(3) clearly made it mandatory for a district council to give notice to each parish council of its intention to pass a resolution to bring the hackney carriage licensing provisions into force for the whole of its area, reading the statute as a whole and recognising the complete lack of prejudice to the defendants from non-compliance with the statutory requirements beyond the fact that non-compliance might give them an argument whereas validity would deprive them of it, if there was substantial compliance with the statutory provision, the act was not invalid).

[Add to end of n.210]

Cf. *R v Stocker* [2013] EWCA Crim 1993; [2014] 1 Cr. App. R. 18.

Marginal failures by individuals to comply with requirements

5–067 *[Add to end of n.240]*

R. *(on the application of Hafeez) v Secretary of State for the Home Department* [2014] EWHC 1342 (Admin) (the fact that H's leave to remain in the United Kingdom expired in November 2011 and his university course finished in January 2012 was not a "near miss" justifying the grant of leave; the absence of a near-miss principle in such cases was well established).

Duties to "have regard to" the desirability of something

5–072 *[Add new n.260a after ". . . persons who do not share it"]*

260a For a summary of the correct approach to be taken to the public sector equality duty, see R. *(on the application of Bracking) v Secretary of State for Work and Pensions* [2013] EWCA Civ 1345; [2014] Eq. L.R. 60 at [25] (McCombe L.J.), followed in R. *(on the application of MA) v Secretary of State for Work and Pensions* [2014] EWCA Civ 13; [2014] P.T.S.R. 584.

5–073 *[Add new para.5–073A after para.5–073]*

5–073A Obligations to "have regard to" may also be created by ministerial guidance: for example, the Secretary of State issued a circular to local authorities under the Local Authority Social Services Act 1970 s.7(1) in which it was said that "councils should have due regard to the actual costs of providing care and other local factors" in setting rates they would pay providers of residential accommodation and care for people for whom the local authorities were responsible. Duties such as this, in a circular or other non-statutory guidance, are not to be equated with statutory duties to "have regard to" and the courts will not "read across" to apply the detailed, structured approach to decision-making developed in relation to the statutory duties.272a

272a R. *(on the application of Members of the Committee of Care North East Northumberland) v Northumberland CC* [2013] EWCA Civ 1740; [2014] P.T.S.R. 758.

Discretionary power in the context of law enforcement

5–079 *[Add to end of n.295]*

(the DPP was required to promulgate an offence-specific policy identifying the facts and circumstances that he would take into account in deciding whether to consent to a prosecution under s.2(1) of the Suicide Act 1961). Cf. *Nicklinson v Ministry of Justice* [2014] UKSC 38; [2014] 3 W.L.R. 200 (the court should not involve itself with the terms of the DPP's policy; it was one thing for the court to decide that the DPP must publish a policy, but quite another for it to dictate what should be in that policy, reversing the Court of Appeal [2013] EWCA Civ 961; [2014] 2 All E.R. 32 on this point).

EXERCISE OF A DISCRETIONARY POWER FOR EXTRANEOUS PURPOSE

Bad faith and improper motive

[Add to end of para.5–084]

In a case concerning the refusal to accept advertisements from a Christian campaign group stating "Not gay! Ex-gay, post-gay and proud. Get over it!", the Court of Appeal held that there was uncertainty as to who had made the refusal decisions—Transport for London (the defendant) or the Mayor of London (not a party); the court ordered further inquiry by the Administrative Court to be conducted as to whether the decision was instructed by the Mayor and whether it was made for the improper purpose of advancing his election campaign.[324a]

[324a] *R. (Core Issues Trust) v Transport for London (Secretary of State for Culture, Media and Sport and Minister for Women and Equalities intervening)* [2014] EWCA Civ 34; [2014] P.T.S.R. 785.

Incidental powers

[Add to para.5–098 after ". . . the discharge of those limited powers.[355]"]   5–098

In *R. (on the application of the National Secular Society) v Bideford Town Council* a parish council's practice of saying prayers as part of the formal business of full meetings of the council was not authorised by s.111 of the 1972 Act.[355a]

[355a] [2012] EWHC 175 (Admin); [2012] 2 All E.R. 1175. See para.5–100 below.

DECISIONS BASED UPON IRRELEVANT CONSIDERATIONS OR
FAILURE TO TAKE ACCOUNT OF RELEVANT CONSIDERATIONS

5–122   *[Add to end of para.5–122]*

In some contexts, written statements of reasons for a decision may be "set out in brief form and their brevity does not indicate a failure to take account of any material considerations".[410a]

[410a] *R. (on the application of Evans) v Cornwall Council* [2013] EWHC 4109 (Admin); [2014] P.T.S.R. 556.

Financial considerations and relevancy

Excessive expenditure

5–137   *[Add to end of para.5–137]*

In *Charles Terence Estates Ltd v Cornwall* CC a local authority raised its own alleged breach of fiduciary duty to its local taxpayers as a defence to an action in private law proceedings for recovery of rent due under lease agreements. The Court of Appeal held that there had been no breach of fiduciary duty but, in any case, such a breach would only render an act ultra vires and void and so provide a defence to a claim in private law if it went to legal capacity.[479a]

[479a] [2012] EWCA Civ 1439; [2013] 1 W.L.R. 466, reversing [2011] EWHC 2542 (QB); [2012] 1 P. & C.R. 2. If the decision of Cranston J. in the High Court was correct then, in the words of Maurice Kay L.J. in the Court of Appeal, Cornwall had succeeded "in ridding itself of what it considered to be bad bargains".

Limited resources

5–138   *[Add to end of n.483]*

Cf. *R. (on the application of Rose) v Thanet Clinical Commissioning Group* [2014] EWHC 1182 (Admin). A 25-year-old woman suffering from Crohn's disease was refused funding for oocyte cryopreservation before undergoing chemotherapy with the probable consequence of infertility and early onset of menopause. R was not considered by T to be clinically exceptional. Jay J., at [113], refused to accept that the policy was a blanket policy that permitted of no exceptions: "In the present case the wording of the exceptionality policy . . . cannot be regarded as potentially discriminatory; the issue is the more limited one of whether it could ever be fulfilled by someone in the claimant's position, and if not whether that matters." An argument based on ECHR arts 8, 12 and 14 also failed.

[Add to para.5–138 after n.485]

Similarly, in *R. (Kebede) v Newcastle City Council,* the Court of Appeal held that a local authority is not permitted to take into account restrictions on its own resources in decision-making under the Children Act 1989 s.23C(4)(b) to give assistance to relevant children "to the extent that his welfare and his educational needs require it".[485a]

[485a] [2013] EWCA Civ 960; [2014] P.T.S.R. 82.

DELEGATION OF POWERS

The Carltona principle

[Add to end of n.592]   5–172

Castle v Crown Prosecution Service [2014] EWHC 587 (Admin); (2014) 178 J.P. 285 (one of the questions posed in an appeal by way of case stated against a speeding conviction was whether an order imposing temporary and variable speed limits was ultra vires because it was signed and/or made by an employee of the Highways Agency (which was not part of the Minister's department); it was held that the *Carltona* principle allowed this delegation of power; the Agency was the alter ego of the Secretary of State in the areas for which he accepted responsibility in Parliament just as he did for the actions of civil servants housed under his departmental roof).

CHAPTER 6

PROCEDURAL FAIRNESS: INTRODUCTION, HISTORY AND COMPARATIVE PERSPECTIVES

THE CONCEPT OF NATURAL JUSTICE

[Add new n.26a after ". . . as phrases which express the same idea"]   6–010

26a These expressions are not always regarded as helpful however. See, eg, *Secretary of State for Communities and Local Government v Hopkins Developments* [2014] EWCA Civ 470 at [48] for concern about use of the expression "fair crack of the whip".

HISTORICAL DEVELOPMENT SINCE THE 1960s

The duty to act fairly

[Add to end of n.174]   6–047

; see also *R. (on the application of L) v West London Mental Health NHS Trust* [2014] EWCA Civ 47; (2014) 158(6) S.J.L.B. 37 at [68], [69] (Beatson L.J. expressing concern that the emphasis on flexibility could lead to an inappropriate drawing together of the concepts of procedural and substantive fairness and undue uncertainty). See also *Secretary of State for Communities and Local Government v Hopkins Developments* [2014] EWCA Civ 470 at [85] ("it does not generally matter whether what is at issue is characterised as 'natural justice' or 'procedural fairness'").

European influences

The ECHR

[Add to end of n.188]   6–048

Where other rights of the Convention are engaged, there may also be procedural requirements specific to the engagement of that particular right. For example, a discussion of the influence of ECHR art.5(4) on procedural requirements in the context of parole board hearings can be found in

Re Reilly's Application for Judicial Review [2013] UKSC 61; [2013] 3 W.L.R. 1020 at [54]–[63] (noting that Convention law permeates the domestic legal system and that domestic law is interpreted and developed in accordance with the Convention as appropriate).

The national security challenge

6–050   *[Add to end of n.194]*

The power may be necessarily implied into the statutory framework: *Bank Mellat v HM Treasury (No. 1)* [2013] UKSC 38; [2014] A.C. 700 at [37]–[43] (since s.40(2) of the 2005 Act provides that an appeal lies to the Supreme Court against "any" judgment of the Court of Appeal, that must extend to parts of a closed judgment as justice will not be able to be done in some cases if the appellate court cannot consider the closed material). For comment, see C. Sargeant, "Two Steps Backward, One Step Forward—the Cautionary Tale of Bank Mellat (No 1)" [2014] 3(1) C.J.I.C.L. 111.

[In para.6–050 delete "at present, it seems likely that Parliament will respond to this judgment by introducing a statutory basis for use of closed material procedures for all civil procedures.[195]" and substitute]

the Justice and Security Act 2013 now extends the possibility of using a CMP to all civil proceedings.[195]

[In n.195 delete "Justice and Security Bill 2012–2013 and"]

CHAPTER 7

PROCEDURAL FAIRNESS: ENTITLEMENT AND CONTENT

SCOPE

[Add to end of n.4] 7–001

Where other rights of the Convention are engaged, there may also be procedural requirements specific to the engagement of that particular right. For example, a discussion of the influence of ECHR art.5(4) on procedural requirements in the context of parole board hearings can be found in *Re Reilly's Application for Judicial Review* [2013] UKSC 61; [2013] 3 W.L.R. 1020 at [54]–[63] (noting that Convention law permeates the domestic legal system and that domestic law is interpreted and developed in accordance with the Convention as appropriate).

ENTITLEMENT TO PROCEDURAL FAIRNESS: OVERVIEW

From "natural justice" to "the duty to act fairly"

[Add to n.17 after ". . . ("simple fairness");"] 7–003

Re Reilly's Application for Judicial Review [2013] UKSC 61; [2013] 3 W.L.R. 1020 at [2], [65]–[71] (reference to "the common law duty to act fairly"); *R. (on the application of L) v West London Mental Health NHS* [2014] EWCA Civ 47; (2014) 158(6) S.J.L.B. 37 at [67] ("the common-law principles of natural justice or fairness").

[Add to n.17 after ". . . [2008] B.L.G.R. 267 at [6]"]

; *Secretary of State for Communities and Local Government v Hopkins Developments* [2014] EWCA Civ 470 at [85] ("it does not generally matter whether what is at issue is characterised as 'natural justice' or 'procedural fairness' ").

[Add to end of n.20]

See also *R. (on the application of LH) v Shropshire Council* [2014] EWCA Civ 404; [2014] P.T.S.R. 1052 at [28] ("the duty to consult will arise when a person has an interest which the law decides is one which is to be protected by procedural fairness").

[Add new n.22a after ". . . the costs of uncertainty"]

[22a] See, e.g. *R. (on the application of L) v West London Mental Health NHS Trust* [2014] EWCA Civ 47; (2014) 158(6) S.J.L.B. 37 at [68], [69] (Beatson L.J. expressing concern that the emphasis on flexibility could lead to an inappropriate drawing together of the concepts of procedural and substantive fairness and undue uncertainty).

[Add to end of n.23]

See also *R. (on the application of L) v West London Mental Health NHS Trust* [2014] EWCA Civ 47; (2014) 158(6) S.J.L.B. 37 (in which the Court of Appeal overturned the procedural requirements specified by the lower court for the decisions of managers of a medium security hospital contemplating referring a detainee to high security conditions as the requirements turned what was largely a clinical decision into an inappropriately adversarial process which went beyond what fairness required).

The recognition of a general duty of fairness

7–009   *[Add to n.49 after ". . . the arbiter of that is fair')"]*

; *Re Reilly's Application for Judicial Review* [2013] U.K.S.C. 61; [2013] 3 W.L.R. 1020 at [64] (the court's function is "not merely to review the reasonableness of the decision-makers judgment of what fairness required"); *R. (on the application of LH) v Shropshire Council* [2014] EWCA Civ 404 at [29] ("[f]airness is a matter for the Court not the Council to decide"); *R. (on the application of Flatley) v Hywel Dda University Local Health Board* [2014] EWHC 2258 (Admin) at [88] ("[i]t is a matter for the court to decide whether a fair procedure was followed").

STATUTORY REQUIREMENTS OF FAIR PROCEDURES

Express statutory requirements

7–011   *[Add to n.56 after ". . . [2006] 1 W.L.R. 3315"]*

; *R. (on the application of Flatley) v Hywel Dda University Local Health Board* [2014] EWHC 2258 (Admin) (limiting the extent of the duty of consultation to that provided for in Community Health Councils (Constitution, Membership and Procedures) (Wales) Regulations 2010 reg.27(7)).

Supplementing statutory procedures

[Add to n.57 after ". . . [2004] EWHC 1220"]   7–012

; *Uprichard v Scottish Ministers* [2013] UKSC 21; [2013] P.T.S.R. D37 at [47]; *Garlick v Secretary of State for Communities and Local Government* [2013] EWHC 1126 (Admin); *Farah v Hillingdon LBC* [2014] EWCA Civ 359; [2014] H.L.R. 24.

[Add to n.59 after ". . . to ensure its fair and workable operation);"]   7–013

Bank Mellat v HM Treasury [2013] UKSC 39; [2014] A.C. 700 at [32] (unless the Act expressly or impliedly excluded any relevant duty of consultation, fairness required an opportunity to make representations before a direction was made);

[Add to para.7–013 after ". . . the courts have supplemented a statutory scheme.⁵⁹"]

Indeed, recently, a majority of the Supreme Court expressed the following view:

> "The duty of fairness governing the exercise of a statutory power is a limitation on the discretion of the decision-maker which is implied into the statute. But the fact that the statute makes some provision for the procedure to be followed before or after the exercise of a statutory power does not of itself impliedly exclude either the duty of fairness in general or the duty of prior consultation in particular, where they would otherwise arise."⁵⁹ᵃ

⁵⁹ᵃ *Bank Mellat v HM Treasury* [2013] UKSC 39; [2014] A.C. 700 at [35].

[In n.60 delete "Bank Mellat v HM Treasury (No.2) [2011] EWCA Civ 1; [2012] Q.B. 101 at [135] (express statutory procedure, including laying instrument before Parliament and right of subsequent judicial review; Parliament had intentionally excluded a duty to hear representations);"]

[Add to end of n.63]

Secretary of State for Communities and Local Government v Hopkins Developments [2014] EWCA Civ 470 at [62] (observing that the Town and Country Planning Appeals (Determination by Inspectors) (Inquiries Procedure) (England) Rules 2000 were *"not a complete code for achieving procedural fairness"*); *R. (on the application of LH) v Shropshire Council* [2014] EWCA Civ 404.

[Add to para.7–013 after ". . . the attainment of fairness'.[63]*"]*

More recently, in *Bank Mellat v HM Treasury*, Lord Sumption observed that he found it hard to envisage cases in which the maximum expression unios exclusion alterius could suffice to exclude so basic a right as that of fairness.[63a]

[63a] [2013] UKSC 39; [2014] A.C. 700 at [35].

7–014   *[In n.66 delete "; Bank Mellat (No. 2) [2011] EWCA Civ 1; [2012] Q.B. 101 at [135]"]*

FAIRNESS NEEDED TO SAFEGUARD RIGHTS AND INTERESTS

7–018   *[Add to end of n.73]*

Re Reilly's Application for Judicial Review [2013] U.K.S.C. 61; [2013] 3 W.L.R. 1020 at [54]–[62], [80]–[96] (noting that a parole board's common law duty to act fairly was influenced by the requirements of ECHR art.5(4) and outlining the circumstances in which oral hearings would be required).

The scope of interests protected by fair procedures

7–023   *[Add to para.7–023 after ". . . proposal to close a local public library?"]*

Does a local authority, having consulted widely on the need to close a certain number of day care centres, owe a specific duty to then consult with users of individual centres?[87a]

[87a] *R. (on the application of LH) v Shropshire Council* [2014] EWCA Civ 404 (finding that a local authority had breached its common law duty in failing to consult with the users of a particular day care centre).

Resource allocation decisions

7–024   *[Add to end of n.94]*

; *Re Reilly's Application for Judicial Review* [2013] UKSC 61; [2013] 3 W.L.R. 1020.

[Add to end of para.7–024]

It has also been held that where a local authority decided to close a day care centre as a result of budgetary constraints, even though there was no express or implied statutory duty to consult, the obligation stemmed from the expectation that a public body, making decisions affecting the public, would act fairly.[96a]

[96a] *R. (on the application of LH) v Shropshire Council* [2014] EWCA Civ 404; [2014] P.T.S.R. 1052 at 21 (Longmore L.J. observing that "[i]f . . . a local authority withdraws a benefit previously afforded to the public, it will usually be under an obligation to consult with the beneficiaries of that service before withdrawing it"; see also [26] (describing the closure as "undoubtedly a serious step")).

FAIR PROCEDURES UNDER ECHR ART 6: THRESHOLD ISSUES

[Add to end of n.115]   7–031

; see also J. Varuhas, "The Reformation of English Administrative Law? Rights, Rhetoric and Reality" [2013] 72(2) C.L.J. 369.

[Add to end of n.123]   7–033

; *Perry v Nursing and Midwifery Council* [2013] EWCA Civ 145; [2013] 1 W.L.R. 3423 at [15]–[16] (assumed though not determined that ECHR art.6 rights were engaged by an interim investigation and suspension decision taken by the Nursing and Midwifery Council).

[Add to n.136 after ". . . Lloyd's Rept. Med. 250 at [33]–[35]"]   7–034

; *Perry v Nursing and Midwifery Council* [2013] EWCA Civ 145; [2013] 1 W.L.R. 3423;

[Add to end of n.136]

Christou v Haringey London Borough Council [2013] EWCA Civ 178.

[Add to end of n.145]

R. (on the application of Ali) v Secretary of State for Justice [2013] EWHC 72 (Admin); [2013] 1 W.L.R. 3536 at [66]–[72] (doubting if a statutory scheme for compensation for reversal of a conviction engaged ECHR art.6).

[Add to end of n.148]

; *R (YA) v Secretary of State for the Home Department* [2013] EWHC 3229 (Admin) at [103] ("not only is it the decision on the part of the administrative authority to refuse leave to an alien to enter but also the decision to impose conditions on an alien's leave to stay which does not involve a determination of civil rights and obligations").

[Add to n.156 after ". . . in the context of financial restrictions"]

(overturned though not on this ground in *Bank Mellat v HM Treasury* [2013] UKSC 39; [2014] A.C. 700). Lord Hope proceeded on the assumption (at [129]) that art.6 applies, albeit that this was not decided.

[Add to n.157 after ". . . interferes with his human rights")]

; see also *Bank Mellat v HM Treasury* [2013] UKSC 39; [2014] A.C. 700 at [157] per Lord Hope (dissenting) ("it is not disputed that the Bank's right to carry on its business was a civil right and that the effect of the direction was to greatly impede the exercise of that right").

FAIR PROCEDURES REQUIRED BY ECHR ART.2: THRESHOLD ISSUES

7–036 *[Add to end of n.168]*

However, where a person detained had committed suicide while in hospital, the State was not required, in fulfilling its procedural obligation under art.2, to perform an immediate and independent investigation into the circumstances of the death prior to an inquest: *R. (on the application of Antoniu) v Central and North West London NHS Foundation Trust* [2013] EWHC 3055; [2014] A.C.D. 44.

[In para.7–036 delete "soldiers of the territorial army, provided they are within the United Kingdom's jurisdiction" and substitute]

those under the authority or control of the state and its agents, as well as those affected a state's agents when exercising authority and control on the state's behalf.

[In n.169 delete from "R (on the application of Smith . . ." and substitute]

Smith v Ministry of Defence [2013] UKSC 41; [2014] A.C. 52. In this case, the Supreme Court took the step of departing from its earlier decision in *R.*

(on the application of Smith) v Oxfordshire Assistant Deputy Coroner (Equality and Human Rights) [2010] UKSC 29; [2011] 1 AC 1. In the earlier case, it had been held that unless they were on a UK military base, British troops on active service overseas were not within the jurisdiction of the United Kingdom. However, in light of the ruling in *Al-Skeini*, the State could be held to exercise jurisdiction extraterritorially wherever the State through its agents exercised control and authority over an individual. See also G. Junor, "A Soldier's (Human) Rights when Fighting Abroad: The Supreme Court Decides" [2013] 37 S.L.T. 251.

[Add to end of n.170]

See also *Smith v Ministry of Defence* [2013] UKSC 41; [2014] A.C. 52 at [65], [75]–[76], [81] in which the Supreme Court held that the extent to which the application of the substantive obligation under art.2 could be held impossible or inappropriate would vary according to context and that procurement decisions, although remote from the battlefield, would not always be appropriate for review. The court had to avoid imposing unrealistic positive obligations on the state regarding the planning and conduct of military operations, but it had to give effect to obligations where it was reasonable to expect the protection of ECHR art.2.

[Add to end of n.171]

; *Keyu v Secretary of State for Foreign and Commonwealth Affairs* [2014] EWCA Civ 312 at [91]–[100] (confirming the continuing application of *In re McKerr* and distinguishing between an inquest which is actually taking place as opposed to the obligation to hold an inquest).

[Add to n.172 after ". . . [2012] 1 AC 725"]

; *McCaughey v United Kingdom* (2014) 58 E.H.R.R. 13.

[In n.172 delete "Janowiec v Russia App. Nos 55508/07 and 29520/09 (April 16, 2012)" and substitute]

Janoweic v Russia (2014) 58 E.H.R.R. 30 at [132]–[133], [144]–[148].

[In n.172 delete "Varnava v Turkey App. Nos 16064/90–16066/90 and 16068/90–16073/90 (September 18, 2009)" and substitute]

Varnava v Turkey (2010) 50 E.H.R.R. 21.

[Add to para.7–036 after ". . . under art.2 applied to the death.[172]"]

However, this obligation appears to only arise in relation to the applicable standards for an ongoing investigation, rather than to the question of whether there is an obligation to commence an investigation into an historic death.[172a]

[172a] *Keyu v Secretary of State for Foreign and Commonwealth Affairs* [2014] EWCA Civ 312 at [91]–[100].

[Add to n.173 after ". . . 49 E.H.R.R. 996 at [163]"]

; *Janoweic v Russia* (2014) 58 E.H.R.R. 30 at [132]–[133].

7–037 *[Add to n.176 after ". . . 28 E.H.R.R. 408 at [100]"]*

; *R. (on the application of Litvinenko) v Secretary of State for the Home Department* [2014] EWHC 194 (Admin); [2014] H.R.L.R. 6 at [50]–[52] (here the ECHR art.2 obligation was discharged by an "extremely thorough" and "exceptionally detailed" police investigation into the death of a man in a London restaurant from radiation poisoning and the attempted extradition of two named suspects).

CONTENT OF PROCEDURAL FAIRNESS: OVERVIEW

A flexible and evolving concept

7–039 *[Add to end of n.183]*

; *Secretary of State for Communities and Local Government v Hopkins Developments* [2014] EWCA Civ 470 (Jackson L.J. noting at [85] that "[f]airness is thus a flexible concept"). However, caution was expressed in respect of an emphasis on procedural fairness being "flexible" in *R. (on the application of L) v West London Mental Health NHS Trust* [2014] EWCA Civ 47; (2014) 158(6) S.J.L.B. 37 at [68]–[69]. Beatson L.J. was concerned that the emphasis could lead to an inappropriate drawing together of the concepts of procedural and substantive fairness and undue uncertainty.

[Add to n.187 after ". . . [2004] 1 A.C. 604"]

Secretary of State for Communities and Local Government v Hopkins Developments [2014] EWCA Civ 470 at [85].

[In n.187 delete "Bank Mellat [2010] EWCA Civ 483; [2012] Q.B. 91" and substitute]

Bank Mellat v HM Treasury [2013] UKSC 39; [2014] A.C. 700.

[Add to end of n.194]   **7–041**

Secretary of State for Communities and Local Government v Hopkins Developments [2014] EWCA Civ 470 at [62] (the Town and Country Planning Appeals (Determination by Inspectors) (Inquiries Procedure) Rules 2000 "are not a complete code for achieving procedural fairness").

PRIOR NOTICE OF THE DECISION

The importance of prior notice

[Add to end of n.200]   **7–043**

R. (on the application of Reilly) v Secretary of State for Work and Pensions [2013] UKSC 68; [2014] A.C. 453 at [65] (invocation of a statutory power in a way which will or may impose a requirement to perform work on a jobseeker allowance claimant and which may have serious consequences on the claimant's ability to meet his or her living needs required the claimant to have access to such information as needed to make an informed and meaningful representation before the decision).

[Add to n.201 after ". . . and, if appropriate, challenge it')"]

(the holding in this case was affirmed in [2014] UKSC 17; [2014] 2 W.L.R. 558 at [28]–[31] on the basis of an interpretation of the relevant statutory provision).

[Add to end of para.7–043]

The Court of Appeal has recently characterised the principle of natural justice or procedural fairness as requiring that any participant in adversarial proceedings is entitled to know the case which he has to meet and to have a reasonable opportunity to adduce evidence and make submissions in relation to that opposing case.[203a]

[203a] *Secretary of State for Communities and Local Government v Hopkins Developments* [2014] EWCA Civ 470 at [47] (holding that it was not a breach of natural justice for a planning inspector to base her decision on issues which emerged in evidence during the course of a planning inquiry but which she had not previously identified as issues in statements produced pursuant to the relevant rules).

[Add to end of n.206]

; *San Vicente v Secretary of State for Communities and Local Government* [2013] EWHC 2713 (Admin); (the grant of planning permission quashed where it was impossible to say what weight the inspector conducting a rehearing of a planning appeal had placed on material from an earlier hearing which was rendered unlawful by a failure to notify objectors; following the procedural defect, a *de novo* hearing should have been held).

The degree of notice required

7–046 *[In n.208 delete "(General Development Procedure) Order 1190 (SI 1995/419)" and substitute]*

(Development Management Procedure) Order 2010 (SI 2010/2184)

Statutory requirements for notice

7–050 *[In n.231 delete "School Organisation (Establishment and Discontinuance of Schools) Regulations 2013" and substitute]*

School Organisation (Establishment and Discontinuance of Schools) Regulations 2013 (SI 2013/3109)

[In para.7–050 delete "a number of interested parties, including: any schools which are proposed to be discontinued;[232] and any local education authority which may be affected by the establishment of the new school.[233] It must also hold at least one public meeting to inform the public of the proposals.[234]" (including footnotes) and substitute]

interested parties that the local authority thinks appropriate.[232]

[232] SI 2013/3109 reg.5(4)(d).

[In para.7–050 delete "in at least one newspaper circulating in the area" and substitute]

on the website of the local authority as well as in both a national and local newspaper

[In n.235 delete "SI 2007/1288 reg.5(1)(h)" and substitute]

SI 2013/3109 reg.5(2)

[In n.236 delete "SI 2007/1288 reg.10(6)(h)" and substitute]

SI 2013/3109 reg.10(4)

Consequences of inadequate notice

[Add to end of n.240]   7–051

See also *Secretary of State for Communities and Local Government v Hopkins Developments Ltd* [2014] EWCA Civ 470 at [62] (noting that if there is procedural unfairness which materially prejudices a party to a planning inquiry that may be a good ground for quashing the Inspector's decision).

CONSULTATION AND WRITTEN REPRESENTATIONS

Standards of consultation

[Add to end of n.245]   7–053

R. (on the application of Flatley) v Hywel Dda University Local Health Board [2014] EWHC 2258 (Admin) at [98] (Community Health Councils (Constitution, Membership and Procedures) (Wales) Regulations 2010 reg.27(7) is solely concerned with the health board's duty to consult with the community health council and not with the public).

[Add to end of n.246]

See also *R. (on the application of LH) v Shropshire Council* [2014] EWCA Civ 404 at [21] (the obligation to consult "requires that there be a proposal, that the consultation takes place before a decision is reached and that responses be conscientiously considered"); *R. (on the application of Flatley) v Hywel Dda University Local Health Board* [2014] EWHC 2258 (Admin) at [88].

[Add to end of n.248]   7–054

; *R. (on the application of Flatley) v Hywel Dda University Local Health Board* [2014] EWHC 2258 (Admin) at [88] (there is no need for a "pre-consultation consultation").

[Delete "although there should be consultation on every viable option" and substitute]

although the decision-maker is entitled to narrow the options prior to consultation, provided the proposed course can still be altered as a result of the consultation, there may be a necessity to deal with alternative options where it would be unfair not to do so.

[Add to beginning of n.249]

R. (on the application of United Company Rusal Plc) v London Metal Exchange [2014] EWCA Civ 1271 (a public body is not required to consult on proposals which it had discarded unless there were very specific reasons for doing so); see also *R. (on the application of M) v Haringey LBC* [2013] EWCA Civ 116; [2013] P.T.S.R. 1285 (in the context of a structured consultation process, fairness did not require consultation on other options which the Council had decided not to incorporate or to explain why those options had not been incorporated, but even had the statutory scheme been less prescriptive and more open-textured, the consultation document's failure to mention other possible ways of meeting the shortfall in funding did not render the process unfair).

[Add to end of n.255]

R. (on the application of Save our Surgery Limited v Joint Committee of Primary Care Trusts [2013] EWHC 439 (Admin); [2013] P.T.S.R. D16 at [27], [109] (sub-scores in assessments of cardiac centres were not "underlying workings" which did not need to be disclosed).

[Add to end of n.265]

R. (on the application of M) v Haringey LBC [2013] EWCA Civ 116; [2013] P.T.S.R. 1285 (announcement of a transitional grant scheme after a consultation for a council tax reduction scheme did not require further consultation as it was not a change of such significance that the council would have been required to draw it to the attention of what would have been a much broader category of consultees than the 36,000 current council tax benefit claimant households in its area).

The increasing importance of consultation

7–056 *[In n.274 delete "http://www.cabinetoffice.gov.uk/resource-library/ consultation- principles-guidance (last accessed December 28, 2012)" and substitute]*

https://www.gov.uk/government/publications/consultation-principles-guidance.

HEARING

[Add to end of n.316]   7–062

Re Reilly's Application for Judicial Review [2013] UKSC 61; [2013] 3 W.L.R. 1020 generally at [80]–[96] and in particular at [85]–[86] (guidance on the necessity for oral hearings before parole boards, which are required in particular where facts which appear to be important are in dispute or where a significant explanation or mitigation is advanced which needs to be heard orally to be accepted, including where an assessment may depend on the view formed by the board of the characteristics of a prisoner which can best be judged by seeing or questioning him in person, where a psychological assessment is disputed or where the board may be materially assisted by hearing evidence, for example, from a psychologist or psychiatrist). For comment, see P. Murray, "Procedural Fairness, Human Rights and the Parole Board" [2014] 73(1) C.L.J. 5.

[Add to end of n.318]

Similarly, if the defendant or his duly authorised advocate agrees (in a voluntary, informed and unequivocal way) that a member of the tribunal can be absent for a part of the hearing and read a transcript of evidence and contribute to the decision, there is no breach of the rules of natural justice: *R. (on the application of Hill) v Chartered Accountants in England and Wales* [2013] EWCA Civ 555; [2014] 1 W.L.R. 86 at [23].

Requirements at an oral hearing

[Add to end of n.321]   7–063

R. (on the application of Hill) v Chartered Accountants in England and Wales [2013] EWCA Civ 555; [2014] 1 W.L.R. 86 at [15] (if it is decided that a defendant or a witness will give oral evidence, then that evidence will be "heard" and it is important that each member of the tribunal should if at all possible "hear" all the evidence; reading the transcript is normally no substitute for hearing evidence from a live witness given oral and for a tribunal member, juror or judge to absent himself without consent while oral evidence is given is usually a breach of the *audi alteram partem* rule).

[Add to n.325 after ". . . [2008] EWCA Civ 811"]   7–064

Bank Mellat v HM Treasury [2013] UKSC 39; [2014] A.C. 700 at [67]–[74].

Adjournments

7–066 *[Add to end of n.331]*

R. *(on the application of Gatawa) v Nursing and Midwifery Council* [2013] EWHC 3435 (Admin) at [18]–[19] (decision not to adjourn a Nursing and Midwifery Council disciplinary hearing to allow more time for a lay representative to prepare on behalf of a nurse, who was suffering from mental illness and was absent, had not been procedurally unfair, where her representative had been given many opportunities to ask for more time).

Failure to appear at an oral hearing

7–068 *[In n.343 delete "Town and Country Planning (Appeals) (Written Representations Procedure) (England) Regulations 2000 (SI 2000/1628)" and substitute]*

Town and Country Planning (Appeals) (Written Representations Procedure) (England) Regulations 2009 (SI 2009/452) as amended by the Town and Country Planning (Appeals) (Written Representations Procedure and Advertisements) (England) (Amendment) Regulations 2013 (SI 2013/2114).

RIGHT TO REASONS

Advantages of a duty to give reasons

7–090 *[Add to end of n.429]*

Secretary of State for the Home Department v CC [2014] EWCA Civ 559 at [38]–[39] (control orders quashed for material non-disclosure where provision of reasons for rejecting abuse allegations in closed judgment prevented the public from knowing the extent to which their allegations had been accepted or rejected).

7–091 *[Add to end of n.432]*

Of course, whether the reasons provided demonstrate error of fact or law is separate from the question of the adequacy of the reasons: see R. *(on the application of C) v Financial Services Authority* [2013] EWCA Civ 677 at [48].

Disadvantages of a duty to give reasons

7–093 *[Add to end of n.438]*

; *Uprichard v Scottish Ministers* [2013] UKSC 21; [2013] P.T.S.R. D37 at [48] (observing that it was important to maintain a sense of proportion when considering the duty to give reasons and not to impose a burden on decision-makers which is unreasonable having regard to the purpose intended to be served and noting that "[i]f the ministers were to be expected to address, line by line, every nuance of every matter raised in every objection, the burden imposed in such circumstances would be unreasonable").

Circumstances in which reasons will be required

To enable an effective right of appeal

[Add to end of n.458]   7–098

; *R. (on the application of T) v Legal Aid Agency* [2013] EWHC 960 (Admin); [2013] 2 F.L.R. 1315 at [14] (fairness dictates that reasons be given for a decision by the Legal Aid Board not to grant prior authority for the preparation of an expert report and an absence of resources did not excuse the lack of reasons).

The standard of reasons required

[In n.490 delete "R. (on the application of C) v Financial Services Authority   7–102
[2012] EWHC 1417; [2012] A.C.D. 97" and substitute]

R. (on the application of C) v Financial Services Authority [2013] EWCA Civ 677 at [44]–[51]

[Add to end of n.497]

; *Uprichard v Scottish Ministers* [2013] UKSC 21; [2013] P.T.S.R. D37 at [48].

ECHR Art.6: Content

Hearing within a reasonable time

[Add to n.579 after ". . . at [108]–[109]"]   7–123

O'Neill v HM Advocate (No 2) [2013] UKSC 36; [2013] 1 W.L.R. 1992 at [25] (noting that art.6(1) of the ECHR contains four separate rights that can and should be considered separately and a complaint that one of them has been breached cannot be answered by showing that the other rights were not breached; see also [36]).

7–125 *[Add new n.586a after "... the stage of the proceedings at which the breach was established"]*

586a See, e.g. *R. (on the application of Sturnham) v Secretary of State for Justice* [2013] UKSC 23; [2013] 2 A.C. 254 (detention beyond a tariff period caused by delay would warrant damages if it could be shown that an earlier hearing would result in earlier release, or had caused sufficiently serious frustration and anxiety).

7–126 *[Add to end of n.589]*

; *Beggs v United Kingdom* (2013) 56 E.H.R.R. 26 (violation of art.6 where appeal proceedings had lasted for over 10 years).

ECHR Art.2: Content

The requirements of art.2

7–127 *[Add to end of n.592]*

; *R. (on the application of Mousa) v Secretary of State for Defence* [2013] EWHC 1412 (Admin); [2013] A.C.D. 84 at [108] and [147].

[Add to para.7–127 after "... to protect their legitimate interests.597"]

It has also been held that an art.2 investigation must encompass broader issues such as planning and control of operations and all surrounding circumstances, not just the actions of State agents who directly used lethal force, and must include "lessons learned" from the identification of wider or systemic issues.597a

597a *R. (on the application of Mousa) v Secretary of State for Defence* [2013] EWHC 1412 (Admin); [2013] A.C.D. 84 at [147].

[Add to para.7–127 after "... collusion in an incident.602"]

Excessive investigative delay will violate ECHR art.2.602a

602a *McCaughey v United Kingdom* (2014) 58 E.H.R.R. 13 at [121]–[140] (prompt response by the authorities in investigating the use of lethal force was essential to maintain public confidence in adherence to the rule of law and in preventing any appearance of collusion in or tolerance of unlawful acts; there had been excessive delay where an inquest began over 21 years after the deaths in question).

[Add to end of para.7–127]

It has been held that there are only two realistic ways in which the State can fulfil its ECHR art.2 obligations in respect of deaths in custody, namely, by setting up an overarching public inquiry or by developing a procedure based on coroner's inquests,[607a] which are now discussed.

[607a] *R. (on the application of Mousa) v Secretary of State for Defence* [2013] EWHC 1412 (Admin); [2013] A.C.D. 84 at [197]–[202], [210] (refusing to direct a public inquiry into deaths of Iraqi civilians in the custody of British armed forces).

[Add to end of n.592]

; *R. (on the application of Mousa) v Secretary of State for Defence* [2013] EWHC 1412 (Admin); [2013] A.C.D. 84 at [108]–[123].

[Add to end of n.596]

; *McCaughey v United Kingdom* (2014) 58 E.H.R.R. 13.

[Add to end of n.602]

See also *R. (on the application of Litvinenko) v Secretary of State for the Home Department* [2014] EWHC 194 (Admin); [2014] H.R.L.R. 6 at [57]–[73] (deficiencies in the reasons "*so substantial*" that a decision for refusing to launch a public inquiry into a death due to radiation poisoning in suspicious circumstances could not stand).

CHAPTER 8

PROCEDURAL FAIRNESS: EXCEPTIONS

EXPRESS STATUTORY EXCLUSION

[In n.15 delete "Criminal Procedure Rules 2002 (SI 2012/1726) r.65.6" and   8–003
substitute]

Criminal Procedure Rules 2002 (SI 2013/1554) r.56.6.

LEGISLATION REQUIRES FAIRNESS FOR SOME BUT NOT OTHER PURPOSES

[Add to end of n.24]   8–005

Bank Mellat v HM Treasury (No.2) [2013] UKSC 39; [2014] A.C. 700 at
[35] (Lord Sumption observing: "Like Lord Bingham in *R (West) v Parole
Board [2005] 1 WLR 350* at para 29, I find it hard to envisage cases in which
the maximum expression unius exclusion alterius could suffice to exclude so
basic a right as that of fairness").

RISK TO THE PUBLIC INTEREST

Risks to national security

[Add to n.40 after ". . . given to that material) at [87]"]   8–007

; *Bank Mellat v HM Treasury (No.1)* [2013] UKSC 38; [2014] A.C. 700 at
[52] (art.6 is the principled control mechanism on what the legislature can
prescribe, and it is for the courts to decide, within parameters set down by
the legislature, how the tension between the need for natural justice and
confidentiality is to be resolved in the natural interest).

[Add to para.8–008 after ". . . restrict such a right⁴⁴"]   8–008

As has recently been observed: "It is no answer that terrorism is horrendous . . . However grave the case, there can come a point where 'the court's sense of justice and propriety is offended'."[44a]

[44a] *Secretary of State for the Home Department v CC and CF* [2014] EWCA Civ 559 at [16] (Kay L.J.).

8–009 *[In n.47 delete "Employment Tribunals (Constitutional and Rule of Procedure) Regulations 2004 (SI 2004/1861) Sch.1, para.54)" and substitute]*

Employment Tribunals (Constitutional and Rule of Procedure) Regulations 2013 (2013/1237) Sch.1, reg.94.

[Add to end of n.48]

Justice and Security Act 2013. See also *R. (on the application of Sarkandi) v Secretary of State for Foreign and Commonwealth Affairs* [2014] EWHC 2359 (Admin) at [30] (in deciding whether an application for public interest immunity rather than a closed material procedure was the more appropriate course, it was necessary to consider whether the claim could fairly be tried without the sensitive material).

[Add to end of n.49]

For a comparative perspective, see A. Gray, "A Comparison and Critique of Closed Court Hearings" [2014] E. & P. 230.

[Add to para.8–009 after ". . . to the other side.[50]*"]*

It has been observed that the process of considering an application to withhold information from disclosure on the grounds of public interest, and the closed material procedure are very different, and in their essence may be thought of as conflicting.[50a]

[50a] *F v Security Service* [2013] EWHC 3402; [2014] 1 W.L.R. 1699 (QB) at [15] (Irwin J. also referring to *Al Rawi v Security Service* [2012] 1 A.C. 531, in which Lord Dyson J.S.C. described (at [41]) a closed procedure as "the very antithesis of PII").

[Add to n.51 after ". . . a substitute for public interest immunity ([192])"]

; *R. (on the application of British Sky Broadcasting Ltd.) v Central Criminal Court* [2014] UKSC 17; [2014] A.C. 885 at [30]–[31].

[In n.51 delete "[2012] EWHC 2837 (Admin)" and substitute]

[2014] EWCA Civ 559

[In para.8–009 delete "although it is not clear" and add after "to conduct a closed material procedure,⁵¹"]

although this does include where the power to conduct a closed material procedure is necessarily implied into the statutory right to appeal decisions where a closed material procedure has been used.[51a] It remains unclear

[51a] *Bank Mellat v HM Treasury (No. 1)* [2013] UKSC 38; [2014] A.C. 700 at [37]–[43] (since s.40(2) of the 2005 Act provides that an appeal lies to the Supreme Court against "any" judgment of the Court of Appeal, that must extend to parts of a closed judgment as justice will not be able to be done in some cases if the appellate court cannot consider the closed material). For comment, see C. Sargeant, "Two Steps Backward, One Step Forward—the Cautionary Tale of Bank Mellat (No 1)" [2014] 3(1) C.J.I.C.L. 111.

[In para 8–009 delete "At the time of writing,⁵³ the Justice and Security Bill 2012–2013 has just passed through Parliament and will extend the possibility of using a CMP to all civil proceedings" and substitute]

The Justice and Security Act 2013 now extends the possibility of using a CMP to all civil proceedings.[53] It is not necessary that a public immunity process be concluded before a closed material procedure.[53a]

[53] For discussion of the Bill as it passed through Parliament, see T. Hickman, "Justice and Security Bill: Defeat or Not a Defeat: That is the Question", UK Const. L. Blog (November 27, 2012). See also, generally J. Jackson, "Justice, Security and the Right to a Fair Trial: Is the Use of Secret Evidence Ever Fair?" (2013) P.L. 720. The central provision in the legislation is s.6, which sets out the conditions in which the court may make a declaration that the proceedings are proceedings in which the closed material application may be made to the court. For application of the legislation, see *CF v Security Service and Mohamed v Foreign and Commonwealth office* [2013] EWHC 3402 (QB); [2014] 1 W.L.R. 1699; *R. (on the application of Sarkandi) v Secretary of State for Foreign and Commonwealth Affairs* [2014] EWHC 2359 at [30] (Admin) (in deciding whether an application for public interest immunity rather than a closed material procedure was the more appropriate course, it was necessary to consider whether the claim could fairly be tried without the sensitive material).

[53a] In *CF v Security Service and Mohamed v Foreign and Commonwealth office* [2013] EWHC 3402 (QB); [2014] 1 W.L.R. 1699 the court made its

first ruling on the use of the Justice and Security Act 2013, accepting that the government could make a closed material application to the court in a civil claim for damages. It was unnecessary that a public immunity process should be concluded before the court accepted a closed material application. The validity of the closed material procedure could not turn on objections which would arise in every case and therefore which would, if successful, subvert Parliament's intention. The courts have criticised the uneasy coexistence of the closed material and public interest immunity procedures (see [2014] 1 W.L.R. at [56]). See also *R. (on the application of Sarkandi) v Secretary of State for Foreign and Commonwealth Affairs* [2014] EWHC 2359 (Admin) at [9] (it was agreed that CPR 82.23(4), which gives effect to s.6 of the legislation and which allows for a hearing in the absence of the specially represented party and the specially represented party's legal representative, ought to be interpreted as allowing such a hearing "so far as necessary").

8–010 *[Add to end of n.54]*

; and the guidance given by the court in *Commissioner of Policy of the Metropolis v Bangs* [2014] EWHC 546 (Admin); (2014) 178 J.P. 158 at [30]–[51], [59] (Beatson J noting at [40] that "[i]n all cases where the issue of PII is raised, what has to be balanced are the public interest which demands the material be withheld as against the public interest in the administration of justice that the individual and the court should have the fullest possible access to all relevant material").

[Add to end of n.56]

Commissioner of Policy of the Metropolis v Bangs [2014] EWHC 546 (Admin); (2014) 178 J.P. 158 at [58].

[Add new n.56a after ". . . in the interests of justice"]

56a However, it has been held that the appropriate question is not whether disclosure "would" result in the harm identified but rather whether there is a real risk of the harm occurring: *Commissioner of Policy of the Metropolis v Bangs* [2014] EWHC 546 (Admin) at [50].

[Add to end of n.57]

; *Bank Mellat* [2013] 4 All E.R. 495 at [68]–[69]; *Bangs* [2014] EWHC 546 (Admin) at [34]–[35], [50]–[51]; *CF v Security Service* [2013] EWHC 3402 (QB); [2014] 1 W.L.R. 1600 at [45]; *Secretary of State for the Home Department v CC and CF* [2014] EWCA Civ 559 (withholding of Secretary of State's case on a potentially dispositive issue and total confinement of reasons for rejecting applicant's case on those issues to the closed judgment invalid).

[Add new n.59a after ". . . especially important"]   8–011

[59a] For discussion of the difference in the balancing in the civil and criminal context, see *Commissioner of Policy of the Metropolis v Bangs* [2014] EWHC 546 at [39]–[40].

[In n.66 delete "[2010] EWCA Civ 483; [2012] Q.B. 91" and substitute]   8–013

Bank Mellat v HM Treasury (No.1) [2013] UKSC 38; [2013] 4 All E.R. 495; *Secretary of State for the Home Department v CC and CF* [2014] EWCA Civ 559 at [16] (use of closed material procedure in abuse of process proceedings against the Secretary of State which would have led to quashing of control orders involved "a radical departure from procedural and constitutional normality" as the closed material procedure limited the obligation of disclosure and permitted much of the detail to be dealt with only in a closed judgment).

[In n.69 delete "Bank Mellat [2011] EWCA Civ 1; [2012] Q.B. 101" and substitute]

Bank Mellat (No.1) [2013] UKSC 38; [2014] A.C. 700 at [5]–[6]; *Secretary of State for the Home Department v CC and CF* [2014] EWCA Civ 559 at [43].

[Add new para.8–013A after para.8–013]

Consideration has also been given recently to the use of a closed material 8–013A
procedure in the appeal context. In *Bank Mellat v HM Treasury (No 2)*, the Supreme Court concluded that, while the Supreme Court rules contained no express power to conduct a closed material procedure, it nonetheless had the power to adopt such a procedure in an appeal under the Counter Terrorism Act 2008 if justice required it and provided guidance on the judicial approach to adopt.[69a]

Meanwhile, the ECJ has suggested that pursuant to art.47 of the Charter of Fundamental Rights of the European Union, the person must be informed of the essence of the grounds which constitute the basis of the decision in question in a manner which takes due account of the necessary confidentiality of the evidence and secondly, to draw, pursuant to national law, the appropriate conclusions from any failure to comply with that obligation to inform him.[69b]

It has also been held that where there has been an open and a closed hearing and a judge gives an open and a closed judgment, it is highly desirable in the open judgment to identify every conclusion in that judgment which has been reached in whole or in part in the light of points made in evidence referred to in the closed judgment and state that this is what has been done.[69c] In addition, where closed material has been relied on, the judge should, in the open judgment, say as much as can properly be said about that closed material.[69d] The principles governing an appeal against an open and closed judgment have recently been considered.[69e] An appellate court should only be asked to conduct a closed hearing if it is strictly necessary for fairly determining the appeal, so that any party who is proposing to invite the appellate court to take such a course should consider very carefully whether it really is necessary to go outside the open material in order for the appeal to be fairly heard.[69f] If the appellate court decides that it should look at closed material, careful consideration should be given by the advocates and the court to the question whether it would nonetheless be possible to avoid a closed substantive hearing.[69g] If a court decides that a closed material procedure appear to be necessary, the parties should try and agree a way of avoiding or minimising the extent of a closed hearing.[69h] If there is a closed hearing, the lawyers representing the party who is relying on the closed material, as well as that party itself, should ensure that, well in advance of the hearing of the appeal: (i) the excluded party is given as much information as possible about any closed documents (including any closed judgment) relied on; and (ii) the special advocates are given as full information as possible as to the nature of the passages relied on in such closed documents and the arguments which will be advanced in relation thereto.[69i] Appellate courts should be robust about acceding to applications to go into closed session or even to look at closed material. Given that the issues will have already been debated and adjudicated upon, there must be very few appeals where any sort of closed material procedure is likely to be necessary. And, in those few cases where it may be necessary, it is hard to believe that an advocate seeking to rely on closed material or seeking a closed hearing, could be unable to articulate convincing reasons in open court for taking such a course.[69j]

[69a] *Bank Mellat v HM Treasury (No.2)* [2013] UKSC 39; [2014] A.C. 700 at [67]–[74].

[69b] *ZZ (France) v Secretary of State for the Home Department (Case C–300/11)* [2013] Q.B. 1136 at [68] (see generally also [53]–[69] for discussion on the EU position).

[69c] *Bank Mellat (No.1)* [2013] UKSC 38; [2014] A.C. 700 at [68].

[69d] *Bank Mellat (No.1)* [2013] UKSC 38; [2014] A.C. 700 at [69].

[69e] *Bank Mellat (No.1)* [2013] UKSC 38; [2014] A.C. 700.

[69f] *Bank Mellat (No.1)* [2013] UKSC 38; [2014] A.C. 700 at [70].

[69g] *Bank Mellat (No.1)* [2013] UKSC 38; [2014] A.C. 700 at [71].

[69h] *Bank Mellat (No.1)* [2013] UKSC 38; [2014] A.C. 700 at [72].

[69i] *Bank Mellat (No.1)* [2013] UKSC 38; [2014] A.C. 700 at [73].

[69j] *Bank Mellat (No.1)* [2013] UKSC 38; [2014] A.C. 700 at [74].
The role of special advocates in closed material procedures

[Add to end of n.70]   8–014

; C. Murphy, "Counter-Terrorism and the Culture of Legality: The Case of Special Advocates" (2013) 24 K.L.J 19.

[Add to end of n.74]   8–015

; *ZZ v Secretary of State for the Home Department* [2014] EWCA Civ 7; [2014] 2 W.L.R. 791 at [37], [39].

[Add to end of n.77]

See also *CC and CF* [2014] EWCA Civ 559; *ZZ (France) v Secretary of State for the Home Department (Case C–300/11)* [2013] Q.B. 1136; [2013] 3 W.L.R. 813; *ZZ (France)* [2014] EWCA Civ 7; [2014] 2 W.L.R. 791 (in the context of the EU Charter of rights, any failure to disclose precisely and in full the grounds on which the decision is based is limited to that which is strictly necessary).

[Add to end of n.80]   8–017

Re CM (EM Country Guidance: Disclosure: Zimbabwe) [2013] EWCA Civ 1303; [2014] Imm. A.R. 326.

SUBSEQUENT FAIR HEARING OR APPEAL

ECHR art.6 and subsequent hearings

[Add to n.164 after ". . . [2011] A.C.D. 86"]   8–037

R. (on the application of Ali) v Secretary of State for Justice [2013] EWHC 72 (Admin); [2013] 1 W.L.R. 3536 at [66]–[72].

[Add to end of n.165]

; *R. (on the application of Ali) v Secretary of State for Justice* [2013] EWHC 72 (Admin); [2013] 1 W.L.R. 3536 at [66]–[72].

LACK OF FAIR PROCEDURE MADE NO DIFFERENCE OR CAUSED NO HARM

8–053   *[Add to end of n.226]*

See also A. Mills, "The 'Makes no Difference' Controversy" [2013] J.R. 124; D. Feldman, "Error of Law and Flawed Administrative Acts" [2014] C.L.J. 275.

Caution required in relation to the "no difference" argument

8–057   *[Add to end of n.242]*

San Vicente v Secretary of State for Communities and Local Government [2013] EWHC 2713 (Admin); [2014] J.P.L. 217 at [29]–[31].

Illustrations

8–059   *[Add to end of n.245]*

See also *R. (on the application of Wilson) v Office of the Independent Adjudicator for Higher Education* [2014] EWHC 558 (Admin); [2014] E.L.R. 273 (lack of mathematical reasoning in arriving at a compensation figure was not an error of law if the ultimate conclusion was within the bracket of reasonable figures which could be arrived at).

[Add to end of n.249]

See also *Burger v Office of the Independent Adjudicator for Higher Education* [2013] EWHC 172 (Admin); [2013] E.L.R. 331 (assessment criteria should have been disclosed to students in advance of an examination; however, non-publication would not have made any difference to complainant's examination performance and would not gain from decision being quashed).

CHAPTER 9

PROCEDURAL FAIRNESS: FETTERING OF DISCRETION

FETTERING OF DISCRETION BY SELF-CREATED RULES OR POLICY

[Add to end of n.7]   9–004

; [2014] UKSC 42 (CAT decision upheld, although the fettering point was not discussed).

Application of the no-fettering principle

[Add to end of n.19]   9–007

Blanket policies may also create human rights challenges. In *R. (on the application of Tigere) v Secretary of State for Business, Innovation and Skills* [2014] EWHC 2452 (Admin) at [26], it was held that a blanket policy of ineligibility for financial support for higher education for all applicants without indefinite leave could not be regarded as justifiable or proportionate and violated ECHR Protocol 1 art.2).

Evidence of a fetter on discretion

[Add to end of n.92]   9–018

; *R. (on the application of Sandiford) v The Secretary of State for Foreign and Commonwealth Affairs* [2014] UKSC 44; *The Times*, July 25, 2014 at [65] (blanket policy under prerogative powers to refuse funding of foreign litigation due to domestic policy and funding considerations not unacceptable).

UNDERTAKING NOT TO EXERCISE A DISCRETION

Common law discretionary powers

[Add to end of para.9–029]   9–029

Similarly, the doctrine does not apply to prerogative powers.[132a]

132a *R. (on the Application of Sandiford) v Secretary of State for Foreign and Commonwealth Affairs* [2014] UKSC 44 at [54], [62] (referring to the reasoning in *R. (on the application of Elias) v Secretary of State for Defence* [2006] EWCA Civ 1293; [2006] 1 W.L.R. 3213, in which it had been held that it is within the power of the decision-maker to decide on the extent to which to exercise a power such as setting up a scheme, it was held that prerogative powers have to be approached on a different basis from statutory powers as there is no necessary implication, from their mere existence, that the State as their holder must keep open the possibility of their exercise in more than one sense).

CHAPTER 10

PROCEDURAL FAIRNESS: BIAS AND CONFLICT OF INTEREST

SCOPE

Introduction

[Add to end of n.1]   10–002

See also *R. (on the application of DM Digital Television Ltd) v Office of Communications* [2014] EWHC 961 (Admin) at [36].

[Add to end of n.10]   10–007

Resolution Chemicals Limited v H Lundbeck A/S [2013] EWCA Civ 1515; [2014] 1 W.L.R. 1943 at [35] ("underlying both article 6 of the Convention and the common law principles is the fundamental consideration that justice should not only be done but should manifestly and undoubtedly be seen to be done").

[Add new n.10a after ". . . and other decision-making bodies"]

10a In this respect, it is important to emphasise that if the fair-minded and informed observer would conclude that there is a real possibility that the tribunal will be biased, the judge is automatically disqualified from hearing the case. The decision to recuse in those circumstances is not a discretionary case management decision reached by weighing various relevant factors in the balance. Considerations of inconvenience, cost and delay are irrelevant: *Resolution Chemicals Limited v H Lundbeck A/S* [2013] EWCA Civ 1515; [2014] 1 WLR 1943 at [35]. A "pragmatic precautionary approach" is required: [40].

HISTORICAL DEVELOPMENT

Gough adjusted: "real possibility"

[Add to para.10–018 after ". . . before the court"]   10–018

73

The notional observer has been described as "something of a paragon. Not only is he fair-minded and impartial, but he has diligently educated himself about the circumstances of the case".[57a]

[57a] *Dar Al Arkan Real Estate Development Company v Majid Al-Sayed Bader Hashim Refai* [2011] EWHC 1055 (COMM) at [37].

[Add to end of n.60]

; see also *R. (on the application of Forge Field Society v Sevenoaks DC* [2014] EWHC 1895 (Admin) at [25] ("The fair-minded observer is neither complacent nor unduly sensitive or suspicious. He views the relevant facts in an objective and dispassionate way").

[Add to end of n.61]

; *O'Neill v HM Advocate (No.2)* [2013] UKSC 36; [2013] 1 W.L.R. 1992 at [53] (the fair-minded and informed observer would be aware that a judge who had made negative comments about two convicted defendants in the context of trial for sexual offences was a professional judge who had taken the judicial oath and had years of relevant training and experience and who would hear and understand the context in which the remarks had been made—namely, in open court, from the bench, while performing his duty as judge and would also appreciate that when the judge was presiding over a second trial against the defendants for murder, he would be doing so in the performance of his duty to preside over that case).

[Add to end of para.10–018]

In similar vein, the courts will also have regard to admissible evidence about what actually happened in the course of the deliberations of the tribunal against which apparent bias is alleged,[66a] and it has been observed that it is important to consider "all of the facts when considering whether apparent bias is established".[66b] Overall, the courts have been keen to emphasise that "[t]he test is not one of 'any possibility' but of a 'real' possibility of bias" and that each case turns on an intense focus on the essential facts of the case.[66c]

[66a] *R. (on the application of DM Digital Television Ltd) v Office of Communications* [2014] EWHC 961 (Admin) at [38], [45]–[47] (observing that, where it is available, it would be wrong in principle to reach a conclusion that there has been apparent bias without having regard to such admissible evidence and holding that the conclusion of a disciplinary panel was supported by the thoroughness of the final decision letters and the notes of the deliberations, which showed that the panel was at pains to address all relevant matters and that no new matters had been introduced in deliberations which the claimant had not had every opportunity to address).

[66b] *R. (on the application of DM Digital Television Ltd) v Office of Communications* [2014] EWHC 961 (Admin) at [37].

[66c] *Resolution Chemicals Ltd v H Hundbeck A/S* [2013] EWCA Civ 1515; [2014] 1 W.L.R. 1943 at [35]–[36] (also noting that a "pragmatic precautionary approach" should guide the approach of the court to applications for recusal: [40]).

AUTOMATIC DISQUALIFICATION FOR BIAS

Great degree of flexibility in application of automatic disqualification

[Add to para.10–031 after ". . . eight years previously did not amount to bias.[100]"]   10–031

In a later case, the fact that a judge was a former pupil of an expert witness who had supervised his university thesis some 30 years previously was not enough to constitute bias in the absence of a continuing link.[100a]

[100a] *Resolution Chemicals Ltd v H Hundbeck A/S* [2013] EWCA Civ 1515; [2014] 1 W.L.R. 1943 at [45]–[49].

[In para.10–031 delete "In a later case" and substitute]

Similarly,

[Add to end of n.101]

; *Resolution Chemicals Limited v H Lundbeck A/S* [2013] EWCA Civ 1515; [2014] 1 W.L.R. 1943 at [46] (the fair-minded and informed observer would not discount the matters of judicial training, experience and ethos).

[Add to end of n.104]

; *Resolution Chemicals Limited v H Lundbeck A/S* [2013] EWCA Civ 1515; [2014] 1 W.L.R. 1943 at [42].

Can automatic disqualification be justified?

[Add to end of n.113]   10–035

However, see *R. (on the application of Shaw) v HM Coroner for Leicester City and South Leicestershire* [2013] EWHC 386 (Admin) (the fully informed

75

independent observer would not have been troubled by a friendship between an assistant deputy coroner and a member of the management of the hospital in which the deceased had died, where the member of management had left the hospital before the deceased's procedure and death).

[Add to end of n.114]

Contrast R. *(on the application of Shaw) v HM Coroner for Leicester City and South Leicestershire* [2013] EWHC 386 (Admin) (no bias arose from the personal friendship between an assistant deputy coroner and the former chief executive of an NHS trust involved in an inquest where the executive had left the post before the incident giving rise to the inquest). In *Shaw*, guidance was provided (at [105]) to coroners where they have an interest which could create apparent bias: disclosure of the interest should be put in writing or otherwise recorded in a permanent record. The coroner should then usually advise any interested person affected of the options: (i) consent to the hearing going ahead and losing the right to object later (waiver); (ii) apply to the coroner to recuse himself (which the coroner will not take amiss), and, if he recuses himself, what effect recusal would have on the timing of the inquest. Any person affected should have adequate time to reflect and, if necessary, take legal or other advice before making a free and informed decision.

Other Situations in which Bias May Occur

Participation in subsequent decision

10–038 *[Add to end of n.116]*

Of course, in almost every case, the judge who heard the substantial application will be the right judge to deal with consequential issues as to costs: *Mengiste v Endowment Fund for the Rehabilitation of Tigray* [2013] EWCA Civ 1003; [2014] P.N.L.R. 4 at [58].

[Add to n.117 after ". . . [2010] PTSR 1527"]

; *O'Neill v HM Advocate (No.2)* [2013] UKSC 36; [2013] 1 W.L.R. 1992 at [53] (the fair-minded observer would appreciate that a judge's comments, although condemning, were made separately in each context, and did not carry over to new decisions. It would only be where the judge had expressed entirely gratuitous opinions that expression of a prior opinion in the judicial context could demonstrate bias).

[Add to end of n.117]

; *Dar Al Arkan Real Estate Development Company v Majid Al-Sayed Bader Hashim Refai* [2014] EWHC 1055 (COMM) [37] (recusal appropriate where the facts informing an earlier and separate decision remained similar).

Illustrations

[In para.10–039 insert two new bullet points after "continue to hold an **10–039** *operator's license.*[125]*" as follows]*

- The fact that a trial judge made adverse comments about defendants at the conclusion of a sexual offences trial would not lead the fair-minded observer to doubt the professional judge's ability to preside over the defendant's subsequent murder trial, unless those comments consisted of entirely gratuitous opinions.[125a]
- A judge who had made two orders against a father for failing to cause the return of his son to the jurisdiction, and had made adverse comments about him and his likely imprisonment, should have recused herself from a committal application.[125b]

[125a] *O'Neill v HM Advocate (No.2)* [2013] UKSC 36; [2013] 1 W.L.R. 1992 at [53]. Contrast *Dar Al Arkan Real Estate Development Co v Majid Al-Sayed Bader Hashim Al Refa* [2014] EWHC 1055 (COMM) at [36]. Smith J. decided to recuse himself from subsequent application where initial decision contained detailed and specific views about the credibility of the witnesses and other crucial issues likely to arise on hearing of the subsequent application, observing as follows: "But it is one thing for the fair-minded and impartial observer to have faith that a judge will reassess his views with an open mind when presented with new evidence and argument. It is asking more of the observer's faith when similar evidence and arguments are presented to assess the same issues. There comes a point when he is entitled to think that, though 'o' independent mind', a judge is 'a man for a' that'. In this case the claimants and Sheikh Abdullatif are entitled to have another judge decide the contempt application."

[125b] *K (A Child)* [2014] EWCA Civ 905 at [56]–[57] (while comments made at earlier hearings were no doubt made to emphasise the importance to the father of complying with court orders and a deep concern for the child's welfare, a fair-minded observer would have been minded to conclude that by April 3, 2014, the judge had made up her mind or was at least strongly disposed to find that the father was in clear breach of the orders requiring him to return or secure the return of the child to the jurisdiction, that those breaches were deliberate and that the father should be given a substantial custodial sentence).

Sub-committees

[Add new para.10–042A after 10–042] **10–042**

10–042A A similar issue has arisen where persons other than the decision-makers are present during the decision-making process.[132a] In this context, a finding of bias can arise where the identity or status of the outsider either does influence the tribunal or would lead a fair-minded person who knows the facts to conclude that there is a real possibility that the tribunal will be influenced.[132b] It seems, however, that a pragmatic approach may be taken to the assistance of outsiders; in *R. (on the application of DM Digital Television Ltd) v Office of Communications*, it was held that it was inevitable that the Board of Ofcom should be assisted by others in the discharge of its regulatory function, as otherwise, the sheer volume of work could not be managed.[132c]

[132a] *R. (on the application of DM Digital Television Ltd) v Office of Communications* [2014] EWHC 961 (Admin) at [32]–[36].

[133b] *R. (on the application of DM Digital Television Ltd) v Office of Communications* [2014] EWHC 961 (Admin) at [36].

[133c] *R. (on the application of DM Digital Television Ltd) v Office of Communications* [2014] EWHC 961 (Admin) at [44].

Relationships

Friendship

10–044 *[Add to para.10–044 after ". . . have been indicative of bias"]*

Similarly, the friendship of an assistant deputy coroner with the former chief executive of an NHS trust involved in an inquest was not indicative of bias where the executive had left the post before the matter giving rise to the inquest arose, and the inquest concerned the hospital's specialist medical team, rather than management.[137a]

[137a] *R. (on the application of Shaw) v HM Coroner for Leicester City and South Leicestershire* [2013] EWHC 386 (Admin).

Professional and vocational relationships

10–046 *[Add to end of n.147]*

See also *Peter Sanders, Brian Ross v Airports Commission, Secretary of State for Transport* [2013] EWHC 3754 (Admin) at [121], [138], [150], [164], [165] (no real possibility of bias where a Commissioner was appointed to a Commission set up to report on airport expansion where the Commissioner had worked as chief executive with a potential purchaser for the airport for

16 years and been involved at the highest level with the potential purchaser for some 22 years, given that the fair-minded and informed observer would be aware that the Commissioner had been retired for almost two years, had been absent from the purchaser's core business and long terms for what would be a lengthy period of time in a dynamic industry; even after the purchaser had announced its intention to purchase, there was nothing to suggest the Commissioner would have been given undue deference and the fair-minded and informed observer would conclude that the Commissioners were a group of people of substance and experience who would regard each other as equals; moreover, the fair-minded and informed observer would have viewed sift criteria as generic criteria developed through an iterative process; however, once proposals were received, the Commissioner was then placed in the position of carrying out a quasi-judicial function of assessing the proposals against sift criteria and the fair-minded and informed observer would have expected him to step down).

[Add to n.149 after ". . . husband's trade union)"]

; *Resolution Chemicals Limited v H Lundbeck A/S* [2013] EWCA Civ 1515; [2014] 1 W.L.R. 1943 at [46] (the fact that an expert witness in the trial of a complex patent action had supervised the doctoral thesis of the specialist High Court judge 30 years previously, where there was no continuing link, did not give rise to apparent bias).

[Add to end of n.159]

See also *R v Connors (Josie)* [2013] EWCA Crim 368; [2013] Crim. L.R. 854 at [34]–[35].

[Add to end of n.161]   10–049

; cf. *R. v Puladian-Kari (Ramin)* [2013] EWCA Crim 158; [2013] Crim. L.R. 510 at [80]–[85] (a fair-minded and informed observer would have concluded that there was a real possibility of bias where a juror passed a note to the judge stating that, in his professional experience, the alleged transaction of the defendant would entail automatic rejection at his institution, and found it difficult to forget details of the case which would be "red signals" in his professional environment).

Personal hostility

[Add to beginning of n.180]   10–054

O'Neill v HM Advocate (No.2) [2013] UKSC 36; [2013] 1 W.L.R. 1992 at [53] (the fair-minded observer would understand the context in which judicial comments were made, and would appreciate that the judge could differentiate his decision in one case from his duty to be impartial in another).

[Add to n.187 after "... of either party held to be vitiating bias);"]

Mengiste v Endowment Fund for the Rehabilitation of Tigray [2013] EWCA Civ 1003; [2014] P.N.L.R. 4 at [58]–[64] (judge who had made trenchant criticisms of the appellant's solicitors should have recused himself as he had expressed his criticisms in absolute terms, failing to leave room for any explanation and had made criticisms at a time when there had been no need to make them to anticipate an application for wasted costs that had not been made).

Pre-determination

10–059 *[Add to n.206 after "... Eu. L.R. 615"]*

; *R. (on the application of Forge Field Society v Sevenoaks DC* [2014] EWHC 1895 (Admin).

SITUATIONS WHERE BIAS WILL NOT APPLY

Waiver

10–061 *[Add to end of n.214]*

O'Neill v HM Advocate (No.2) [2013] UKSC 36; [2013] 1 W.L.R. 1992 at [56] (failure to object may also indicate to the fair-minded observer that the parties did not consider that there was indeed an existence of bias); *R. (on the application of DM Digital Television Ltd) v Office of Communications* [2014] EWHC 961 (Admin) at [41]. It was also held in this case that waiver can be inferred from conduct or even silence, provided that the conduct or silence is voluntary, informed and unequivocal: at [43]. See also *R. (on the application of Shaw) v HM Coroner for Leicester City and South Leicestershire* [2013] EWHC 386 (Admin) at [101].

ECHR ART.6

10–090 *[Add to end of n.291]*

; see also *Resolution Chemicals Limited v H Lundbeck A/S* [2013] EWCA Civ 1515; [2014] 1 W.L.R. 1943 at [35] ("underlying both article 6 of the

Convention and the common law principles is the fundamental consideration that justice should not only be done but should manifestly and undoubtedly be seen to be done").

[Add new para.10–091A after para.10–091]   **10–091**

The obligation in ECHR art.6 to ensure access to independent and impartial **10–091A**
courts for the resolution of "civil rights and obligations" imposes an obligation on states to respect the court process and to comply with judgments
delivered by the courts. This means that contracting states cannot legislate in
a manner which affects the judicial determination of a dispute involving the
State or private parties; such an intervention by the executive is only permis-
sible on compelling grounds of the public interest. Thus, in *R. (on the application of Reilly) (No 2) v Secretary of State for Work and Pensions,*[297a] the
Jobseekers (Back to Work Schemes) Act 2013 was declared to be incompatible with the ECHR as it retrospectively validated the Jobseeker's Allowance
(Employment, Skills and Enterprise Scheme) Regulations 2011. The 2011
Regulations had imposed sanctions of withholding of benefit on those who
refused to participate in the scheme, and they had been held invalid by the
Court of Appeal. The 2013 Act retrospectively validated both the 2011
Regulations and the sanctions imposed pursuant to them. The court was not
persuaded that there were compelling grounds of the general interest to
justify the interference with art.6(1) rights of the claimants to a judicial
determination of their claims.

[297a] [2014] EWHC 2182 (Admin).

CHAPTER 11

SUBSTANTIVE REVIEW AND JUSTIFICATION

INTRODUCTION

Overlap between unreasonableness and proportionality

[Add to n.23 after "... 'Problems and Proportionality' [2010] N.Z.L.R. **11–010**
303;"]

See also J. Goodwin, "The Last Defence of Wednesbury" [2012] P.L. 445.

Constitutional and institutional limitations on the court's role

[Add to end of n.39]   **11–014**

*R. (on the application of Lord Carlile of Berriew) v Secretary of State for the
Home Department* [2013] EWCA Civ 199 (refusal to allow the entry of a
dissident Iranian politician into the United Kingdom) at [75] per Arden L.J.:
"For me to conclude that these concerns are irrational would . . . involve
substituting my own judgment for that of the Secretary of State . . . [whose]
decision requires expertise in evaluating the current and historical evidence
and in predicting the reaction of the Iranian regime. It also requires up to
date intelligence as to the likely response." In *Bank Mellat v HM Treasury*
[2013] UKSC 39; [2013] 3 W.L.R. 179 (Order in Council prohibiting transactions or business relationships with Iranian Bank to prevent development
of nuclear weapons in Iran) at [21] Lord Sumption cautioned against the
court taking over the functions of the executive, least of all in the area of
foreign policy and national security "which would once have been regarded
as unsuitable for judicial scrutiny"; the question whether a measure was apt
to limit the risk posed for the national interest by nuclear proliferation was
"pre-eminently a matter for the executive". He endorsed the view of Lord
Reed that "the making of government and legislative policy cannot be turned
into a judicial process". Lord Sumption, in a majority of five to four, nevertheless allowed the Bank's appeal on the ground, inter alia, that the Order in
Council was not a rational or proportionate response to the aim of hindering
Iran's nuclear ambitions.

Courts' secondary function of testing the quality of reasoning and justification

11–016 *[Add new n.43a after ". . . the situation in immigration policy where those elements were not present"]*

43a But see *R. (on the application of MM (Lebanon)) v Secretary of State for the Home Department* [2014] EWCA Civ 985 (where the Court of Appeal was persuaded as to the Secretary of State's proposed "Minimum Income Requirement" for a UK partner to sponsor the entry of a non-EEA partner) at [148] per Aikens L.J.: ". . . appropriate weight has to be given to the judgment of the Secretary of State, particularly where, as here, she has acted on the results of independent research and wide consultations".

THE WEDNESBURY FORMULATION AND ITS SUBSEQUENT DEVELOPMENT

Wednesbury is tautological

11–020 *[Add new n.56a after ". . . in the minds of reasonable men."]*

56a Lord Russell's formulation was approved by Aikens L.J.in the context of a challenge to immigration rules in *R. (on the application of MM (Lebanon)) v Secretary of State for the Home Department* [2014] EWCA Civ 985 at [94]–[95].

UNREASONABLE PROCESS

Inadequate evidence and mistake of fact

Decisions unsupported by substantial evidence

11–052 *[Add to end of n.145]*

R. (on the application of Trafford) v Blackpool BC [2014] EWHC 85; [2014] 2 All E.R. 947 (see n.259 below) (no evidence that the nature of a solicitor's business whose lease the defendant council refused to renew was "wholly contrary to the stated aims and objectives" of the council).

VIOLATION OF COMMON LAW RIGHTS OR CONSTITUTIONAL PRINCIPLE

The common law principle of equality

The rule of law

[Add to end of para.11–061]

Retrospective legislation also violates the rule of law in the absence of very **11–061** strong justification.[180a]

[180a] *R. (on the application of Reilly (No.2) and Hewstone) v Secretary of State for Work and Pensions* [2014] EWHC 2182 (Admin) (the Jobseeker's (Back to Work Schemes) Act 2013 sought to retrospectively validate the 2011 Jobseeker's Allowance (Employment, Skills and Enterprise Scheme) Regulations, notification letters that had failed to comply with those regulations and sanctions which had been imposed pursuant to the regulations; the court granted a declaration of incompatibility) at [82] per Lang J.: "The constitutional principle of the rule of law was expressly recognised in section 1, Constitutional Reform Act 2005. It requires, *inter alia*, that Parliament and the Executive recognise and respect the separation of powers and abide by the principle of legality. Although the Crown in Parliament is the sovereign legislative power, the Courts have the constitutional role of determining and enforcing legality. Thus, Parliament's undoubted power to legislate to overrule the effect of court judgments generally ought not to take the form of retrospective legislation designed to favour the Executive in ongoing litigation in the courts brought against it by one of its citizens, unless there are compelling reasons to do so. Otherwise it is likely to offend a citizen's sense of fair play." See also para.1–033 nn.94 and 105.

Substantive equality

[Add to end of n.202]   11–067

The UK government has not signed ECHR Protocol 12, which contains a free-standing prohibition of discrimination. See para.13–030 below.

OPPRESSIVE DECISIONS

Illustrations of oppressive decisions

[Add to end of n.259]   11–072

See also *R. (on the application of Trafford) v Blackpool BC* [2014] EWHC 85; [2014] 2 All E.R. 947 (decision not to renew solicitor's business tenancy because the solicitor had acted for a number of clients who had brought personal injury claims against the council held to be unlawful) at [71] per H.H. Judge Stephen Davies: "The exercise of a power with the sole or the dominant intention of punishing the claimant . . . in circumstances where there was no evidence that the claimant was actually doing anything at all unlawful or improper, was . . . the intentionally improper exercise of the power . . . and the exercise of that power for unauthorised purposes."

[Add to end of n.262]

See also *R. (on the application of MM (Lebanon)) v Secretary of State for the Home Department* [2014] EWCA Civ 985, [150] (reversing [2013] EWHC 1900 (Admin); [2014] 1 W.L.R 2306) (challenge to a "Minimum Income Requirement" for a UK partner to sponsor the entry of a non-EEA partner) at [147]–[148] per Aikens L.J.: "Essentially the debate is about figures and what should be the minimum necessary income figure and what other possible sources of income should or should not be taken into account to see if that minimum can be reached . . . the key question is: to what extent should the court substitute its own view of what, as a matter of general policy, is the appropriate level of income for that rationally chosen as a matter of policy by the executive, which is headed by ministers who are democratically accountable? . . . Individuals will have different views on what constitutes the minimum income requirements needed to accomplish the stated policy aims . . . it is not the court's job to impose its own views unless, objectively judged, the levels chosen are . . . irrational, or inherently unjust or inherently unfair."

THE PLACE OF PROPORTIONALITY

11–074 *[Add to end of n.271]*

See Lord Neuberger P.S.C., "The Role of Judges in Human Rights Jurisprudence: A Comparison of the Australian and UK Experience" (conference speech given at the Supreme Court of Victoria, Melbourne, August 8, 2014, available at *http://www.supremecourt.uk/docs/speech-140808.pdf*) para.31): ". . . we now have new ideas to grapple with and to apply to our domestic law, such as the concept of proportionality. But we are also wondering whether . . . it makes sense to have such different approaches between a traditional JR challenge to an executive decision on the merits, and a Convention challenge to an administrative decision. On that issue, the judgment in *Kennedy (Kennedy v Charity Commission* [2014] UKSC 20; [2014] 2 W.L.R. 808) has something to offer."

Proportionality as a structured test of justifiability

Structured proportionality in Convention rights

[Add to end of n.287]   11–079

In *Bank Mellat v HM Treasury* [2013] UKSC 39; [2013] 3 W.L.R. 179 at
[70], [72] Lord Reed commented that the European Court of Human Rights
often approached striking a fair balance "in a relatively broad-brush way . . .
The intensity of review varies considerably according to the right in issue
and the context in which the question arises. Unsurprisingly . . . its approach
to proportionality does not correspond precisely to the various approaches
adopted in contracting states". Further, on the approach to proportionality
adopted in the UK domestic courts under the Human Rights Act, he
continued: "In accordance with the analytical approach to legal reasoning
characteristic of the common law, a more clearly structured approach has
generally been adopted."

Structured proportionality in English law

[Add to end of n.294]   11–081

In *Bank Mellat v HM Treasury* [2013] UKSC 39; [2013] 3 W.L.R. 179 at [74]
Lord Reed, in a statement approved by the whole court, said that the
approach in *Oakes* could be summarised by saying that it is necessary to
determine: "(1) whether the objective of the measure is sufficiently important to justify the limitation of a protected right, (2) whether the measure is
rationally connected to the objective, (3) whether a less intrusive measure
could have been used without unacceptably compromising the achievement
of the objective, and (4) whether, balancing the severity of the measure's
effects on the rights of the persons to whom it applies against the importance
of the objective, to the extent that the measure will contribute to its achievement, the former outweighs the latter." Further, ". . . there is a meaningful
distinction to be drawn . . . between the question whether a particular objective is in principle sufficiently important to justify limiting a particular right
(step one), and the question whether, having determined that no less drastic
means of achieving the objective are available, the impact of the rights
infringement is disproportionate to the likely benefits of the impugned
measure (step four)" (at [76]). Lord Sumption also acknowledged the fourth
step in his leading judgment as requiring "a fair balance . . . between the
rights of the individual and the interests of the community" (at [20]). In *R.
(on the application of Miranda) v Secretary of State for the Home Department*
[2014] EWHC 255 (Admin); [2014] 3 All E.R. 447 at [40] Laws L.J. said of
the *Oakes* fourth step: "I think it needs to be approached with some care. It
requires the court . . . to decide whether the measure, though it has a

justified purpose and is no more intrusive than necessary, is nevertheless offensive because it fails to strike the right balance between private right and public interest; and the court is the judge of where that balance should lie . . . there is real difficulty in distinguishing this from a political question to be decided by the elected arm of government. If it is properly within the judicial sphere, it must be on the footing that there is a plain case." On the facts of that case, however, the balance was to be struck between two aspects of the public interest—press freedom and national security—and, on the facts, the balance clearly favoured national security.

INTENSITY OF REVIEW

11–086 *[Add to n.310 after ". . . the minimum interference test, counselled its "cautious deployment");"]*

The Court of Appeal's decision was reversed by the Supreme Court [2013] UKSC 39; [2013] 4 All E.R. 533. In his leading judgment, however, Lord Sumption stated at [20] that he agreed with the view expressed in the court below by Maurice Kay L.J. that "this debate [on minimum interference] is sterile in the normal case where the effectiveness of the measure and the degree of interference are not absolute values but a question of degree, inversely related to each other. The question is whether a less intrusive measure could have been used without unacceptably compromising the objective". Lord Reed commented at [75]: "In relation to (the minimum interference test) Dickson CJ made clear in *R v Edwards Books and Art Ltd* [1986] . . . that the limitation of the protected right must be one that "it was reasonable for the legislature to impose", and that the courts were "not called on to substitute judicial opinions for legislative ones as to the place at which to draw a precise line." This approach is unavoidable, if there is to be any real prospect of a limitation on rights being justified: as Blackmun J once observed, "a judge would be unimaginative indeed if he could not come up with something a little less drastic or a little less restrictive in almost any situation, and thereby enable himself to vote to strike legislation down".

[Add to end of n.314]

See also *SS (Nigeria) v Secretary of State for the Home Department* [2013] EWCA Civ 550; [2014] 1 W.L.R. 998 at [41]–[42] per Laws L.J.: "But the principle [of minimal interference] does *not* tell us that . . . the court must always be the primary judge of the principle's fulfilment or otherwise. The court insists that the decision-maker respect the principle; but this is perfectly consonant with the decision-maker's enjoyment of a margin of discretion as to what constitutes minimal interference. . . . the breadth of this margin is conditioned by context, and in particular driven by two factors: (1) the nature of the public decision, and (2) its source . . . The principle . . . can never . . . be treated as a token or ritual. But the margin of discretionary judgment enjoyed by the primary decision-maker, though variable, means that the court's role is kept in balance with that of the elected arms of government." See A. Vaughan, "Minimum Interference Versus Rationality: The New Battleground in HRA Proportionality?" [2013] J.R. 416.

CHAPTER 12

LEGITIMATE EXPECTATIONS

INTRODUCTION

Legitimate expectations of procedural fairness

Secondary procedural legitimate expectation

[Add to n.20 after "[2008] EWCA Civ 755;"]   **12–011**

(2008) 152(29) S.J.L.B. 29;

Illustrations

[Add to end of n.35]   **12–015**

In *R. (on the application of LH) v Shropshire Council* [2014] EWCA Civ
404; (2014) 17 C.C.L. Rep. 216, the *Baker* principle was applied in the
context of the closure of adult day care centres. In *LH* the council had
engaged in a general consultation process on reorganisation of day centres
across the county but the issue was whether there should have been specific
consultation about the closure of Hartleys Day Centre, used by LH. Informed
by that general consultation, the council then decided which particular day
centres to close. The Court of Appeal, reversing the Administrative Court
decision [2013] EWHC 4222 (Admin), concluded that the fairness of the
procedure was for the court to decide and although the council had initially
undertaken wide-ranging consultation it should have mounted a fresh
consultation in relation to any individual day centre it then sought to close;
R. (on the application of Save our Surgery Ltd [2013] EWHC 439 (Admin);
[2013] Med. L.R. 150 (consultation process for identification of seven
specialist centres in England for the future performance of paediatric cardiac
surgery declared unfair; in the subsequent determination of what relief to
grant the claimant, the court granted a quashing order but declined to dictate
what steps should be taken because it had neither the requisite knowledge or
expertise: [2013] EWHC 1011 (Admin); [2013] Med. L.R. 172).

[Add additional bullet point at end of para.12–015]

- A person qualifying as a doctor could rely on clear, unequivocal and unqualified assurances from the GMC that if he completed his proposed distance learning course of study in a reasonable time his qualification would be recognised even though the registration criteria had been changed before completion.[40a]

[40a] *R. (on the application of Patel) v General Medical Council* [2013] EWCA Civ 327; [2013] 1 W.L.R. 2801, reversing [2012] EWHC 2120 (Admin); (2012) 128 B.M.L.R. 146.

THE SOURCE OF A LEGITIMATE EXPECTATION

12–016 *[Add new n.41a after "The representations which induce a legitimate expectation can thus be express or implied"]*

[41a] See F. Ahmed and A. Perry, "The Coherence of the Doctrine of Legitimate Expectations" [2014] C.L.J. 61 for a rule-based account of why certain promises, practices and policies give rise to legitimate expectations whereas others do not.

LEGITIMACY

12–030 *[Add new n.88a after ". . . must possess the following qualities"]*

[88a] In *United Kingdom Association of Fish Producer Organisations v Secretary of State for the Environment, Food and Rural Affairs* [2013] EWHC 1959 (Admin) at [92] Cranston J. said:

> "[T]he threads of the English doctrine of substantive legitimate expectation can be drawn together in the following propositions: 1. The undertaking must be clear, unambiguous and without relevant qualification: *Bancoult*, [60]. 2. On ordinary principles an undertaking can derive from a representation or a course of conduct. However, the mere existence of a scheme is inadequate in itself to generate a substantive legitimate expectation: *Bhatt Murphy*, [63]. 3. Whether there is such an undertaking is ascertained by asking how, on a fair reading, the representation or course of conduct would reasonably have been understood by those to whom it was made: *Patel*, [44]–[45], applying *Paponette*, [30]. 4. Although in theory the defined class being large is no bar to their having a substantive legitimate expectation, in reality it is likely to be small if the expectation is to be made good: *Bhatt Murphy*, [46]. In *Paponette* the successful class to whom a collective promise had been made was some 2,000. 5. Detrimental reliance is not an essential requirement. However, it may be necessary where the issue is in the

macro-political field or a person-specific undertaking is alleged: *Bancoult*, [60]; *Begbie*, 1124 B-C, 1133 D-F. 6. To justify frustration of a substantive legitimate expectation, the decision maker must have taken into account as a relevant consideration the undertaking and the fact that it will be frustrated: *Paponette*, [45]–[46]. 7. Legitimate expectation is concerned with exceptional situations: *Bhatt Murphy*, [41]. 8. Justification turns on issues of fairness and good administration, whether frustrating the substantive legitimate expectation can be objectively justified in the public interest and as a proportionate response. Abuse of power is not an adequate guide: *Nadarajah*, [70]. 9. The intensity of review depends on the character of the decision. There will be a more rigorous standard than *Wednesbury* review, with a decision being judged by the court's own view of fairness. A public body will not often be held bound to maintain a policy which on reasonable grounds it has chosen to change. There will be less intrusive review in the macro-political field. As well, respect will be accorded to the relative expertise of a decision-maker: *Bhatt Murphy*, [35], [41]; *Patel*, [60]–[62], [83]. 10. Transitional arrangements, and whether there has been a warning of possible change, are not essential but may be relevant to the court's assessment of justification: *Bhatt Murphy* [18]–[20], [56]–[57], [60]–[61], [65]–[70]; *Patel*, [77], [83]."

Clear, unambiguous and devoid of relevant qualification

[Add to end of n.89]   **12–031**

R. (on the application of Lewisham LBC v Assessment and Qualifications Alliance (AQA) [2013] EWHC 211 (Admin); [2013] E.L.R. 281 (assurance relied upon not sufficiently unequivocal to create a legitimate expectation that GCSE grade boundaries would not change from one assessment point to the next); *United Kingdom Association of Fish Producer Organisations v Secretary of State for the Environment, Food and Rural Affairs* [2013] EWHC 1959 (Admin) (no clear, unambiguous and without qualification undertaking by the Secretary of State that the fishing fixed quota allocation system adopted for the past 13 years would continue in its existing form; the representations amounted to no more than an explanation as to how the system operated).

When is the Disappointment of a Substantive Legitimate Expectation Unlawful?

[Add to end of n.145]   **12–046**

R. (on the application of Alansi) v Newham LBC [2013] EWHC 3722; [2014] B.L.G.R. 138 (a change of housing policy resulting in A losing her status as a priority home seeker was a proportionate response to a pressing and widespread social problem despite a prior clear and unequivocal assurance that A would retain her priority status if she took up a private rented tenancy which the new policy then excluded from priority status).

12–047 *[Add to end of para. 12–047]*

In *Patel*, the Court of Appeal held that the GMC had to honour a clear, unequivocal and unqualified assurance given to P that if he completed his distance-learning course of study in a reasonable time, his qualification would be recognised. This was not outweighed by any prevailing public interest; transitional arrangements should have been put in place.[147a]

[147a] *R. (on the application of Patel) v General Medical Council* [2013] EWCA Civ 327; [2013] 1 W.L.R. 2801.

THE STANDARD OF JUDICIAL REVIEW

12–052 *[Add to end of n.160]*

In *R. (on the application of Patel) v General Medical Council* [2013] EWCA Civ 327; [2013] 1 W.L.R. 2801 at [83], Lloyd Jones L.J. held: "When the court considers the fairness of overriding a substantive legitimate expectation, the standard of review is a sliding scale . . . Normally, the court would accord a considerable degree of respect to a specialist body such as the GMC which is required by Parliament to decide what qualifications should be recognised." But: (i) there was no reason to conclude that distance learning was such a problem as to demand immediate withdrawal of recognition without any steps to mitigate the impact of such a decision; (ii) the expectation was founded upon an express statement rather than a former policy or course of conduct; (iii) the representation was made to an individual personally; (iv) the expectation was of high importance to P; (v) detrimental reliance was present in abundance; and (vi) the decision of the GMC was not in the macro-political field.

The subject matter of the representation

12–055 *[Add to end of n.176]*

Cf. *R. (on the application of Patel) v General Medical Council* [2013] EWCA Civ 327; [2013] 1 W.L.R. 2801 (expectation that undertaking an existing distance learning course would lead to recognition of the qualification awarded in the future).

Degree of reassurance

[Insert new n.179a after "... as much weight as an oral or written **12–057** *representation"]*

179a R. *(on the application of Patel) v General Medical Council* [2013] EWCA Civ 327; [2013] 1 W.L.R. 2801.

Nature of the decision

[Add to end of n.182] **12–058**

See also R. *(on the application of Patel) v General Medical Council* [2013] EWCA Civ 327; [2013] 1 W.L.R. 2801.

Detrimental reliance

[Add to end of n.185] **12–059**

R. *(on the application of Patel) v General Medical Council* [2013] EWCA Civ 327; [2013] 1 W.L.R. 2801 (course undertaken in expectation that it would lead to a recognised qualification was extremely demanding in terms of time and effort with a total financial cost of some US$40,000).

CHAPTER 13

CONVENTION RIGHTS AS GROUNDS FOR JUDICIAL REVIEW

PROTECTION OF FUNDAMENTAL RIGHTS IN DOMESTIC AND INTERNATIONAL LAW

The Council of Europe

[Add to end of n.14]   13–006

The total number of pending applications on June 30, 2014 was 84,850, a fall of 15 per cent from the same stage in 2013 (see *http://www.echr.coe.int/ Documents/Stats_month_2014_ENG.pdf*). Two further Protocols have been adopted but not yet entered into force: Protocol 15 would give effect to the proposed reduction in the time limit for bringing proceedings in art.35 of the ECHR from six months to four and would introduce references in the Preamble to the ECHR to the principles of subsidiarity and the margin of appreciation; and Protocol 16 would permit the highest courts of state parties to request an advisory opinion relating to the interpretation or application of Convention rights (on which, see K. Dzehtsiarou and N. O'Meara, "Advisory Jurisdiction and the European Court of Human Rights: A Magic Bullet for Dialogue and Docket Control?" (2014) 34 L.S. 444).

[In n.19 delete final sentence and substitute]   13–007

Four such Guides have so far been published: on arts 4, 5, and 6 (civil and criminal). Of the applications pending before the ECtHR in June 2014, 13.7 per cent are against Russia, 12.1 per cent are against Turkey, 19 per cent are against the Ukraine, and 18.1 per cent are against Italy. In the first six months of 2014, some 48,354 applications were decided, a slight fall from the same period in 2013 but a significant increase from 1995. For up-to-date statistics, see *http://www.echr.coe.int/Pages/home.aspx?p=reports*.

THE EUROPEAN CONVENTION ON HUMAN RIGHTS

[Add to end of n.21]   13–009

See now C. Grabenwarter, *The European Convention on Human Rights: A Commentary* (2013).

Derogations

13–023 *[Add to end of n.47]*

Art.15 must be read as applying to the extraterritorial jurisdiction of the Convention: *Mohammed v Ministry of Defence* [2014] EWHC 1369 (QB) at [155]–[157] (doubting the dictum in *Al-Jedda v Secretary of State for Defence* [2007] UKHL 58; [2008] 1 A.C. 332 at [38]). *Mohammed* concerned a successful claim for a violation of art.5 by an Afghan national detained for over 100 days by British forces in Afghanistan without any lawful authority (beyond the first 96 hours).

Interpreting the ECHR

13–029 *[Add to end of n.60]*

In *Vallianatos v Greece* (2014) 59 E.H.R.R. 12 at [91], the ECtHR acknowledged the trend emerging in the legal systems of the Council of Europe (which has yet to reach consensus) to recognise same-sex relationships. A 2008 Greek law which excluded same-sex couples from forming civil unions was a breach of art.8 read with art.14.

13–030 *[Delete first sentence of para.13–030 and substitute]*

The Council of Europe has adopted a total of 16 Protocols.

THE HUMAN RIGHTS ACT 1998

The authority of Strasbourg decisions

13–036 *[Add to end of n.82]*

Lines of Strasbourg authority may become less clear over time. However, the fact that there may be a "direction of travel" in Strasbourg jurisprudence which appears to depart from a formerly stated principle will not allow for that principle to be replaced with a "new interpretation" without "a clear, high level exegesis of the salient principle and its essential components": *Kennedy v Charity Commission* [2014] UKSC 20; [2014] 2 W.L.R. 808 at [145]–[108]. In *Kennedy*, the SC held that there was no art.10 right to receive information from public authorities: see para.13–090.

[Add to end of n.85]

The CA has summarised the above authorities and the more recent SC cases of *R. (on the application of Osborn) v Parole Board* [2013] UKSC 61; [2013] 3 W.L.R. 1020 at [56]–[57] and *R. (on the application of Chester) v Secretary of State for Justice* [2013] UKSC 63; [2014] A.C. 271 at [27], [120]–[124] in the following principles: (1) it is the duty of the national courts to enforce domestically enacted Convention rights; (2) the ECtHR is the court that, ultimately, must interpret the meaning of the Convention; (3) the UK courts will be bound to follow an interpretation of a provision of the Convention if given by the Grand Chamber as authoritative, unless it is apparent that it has misunderstood or overlooked some significant feature of English law or practice which, properly explained, would lead to that interpretation being reviewed by the ECtHR when its interpretation was being applied to English circumstances; (4) the same principle and qualification applies to a "clear and constant" line of decisions of the ECtHR other than one of the Grand Chamber; (5) Convention rights have to be given effect in the light of the domestic law which implements in detail the "high level" rights set out in the Convention; and (6) where there are "mixed messages" in the existing Strasbourg case law, a "real judicial choice" will have to be made about the scope and application of the relevant provision of the Convention (*R. (on the application of Hicks) v Commissioner of Police of the Metropolis* [2014] EWCA Civ 3; [2014] 1 W.L.R. 2152 at [80]). In *Hicks*, the CA declined to follow the recent decision of the ECtHR in *Ostendorf v Germany* (App. No.15598/08) (March 7, 2013) on the basis that it was not consistent with the ECtHR's earlier case law. See further n.170.

[Add to end of n.86]

The CA granted permission to appeal to the SC in *R. (on the application of Kaiyam) v Secretary of State for Justice* [2013] EWCA Civ 1587; [2014] 1 W.L.R. 1208 rather than follow the ECtHR's decision in *James, Wells and Lee v UK* (2013) 56 E.H.R.R. 12 (see n.191).

Declaration of incompatibility

[Delete all text in n.112 and substitute]   13–047

See Table 1 at the end of this Chapter for a summary of the declarations of incompatibility made up to the end of August 2014.

[Add to end of n.115]   13–048

In *R. (on the application of Nicklinson) v Ministry of Justice* [2014] UKSC 38; [2014] 3 W.L.R. 200, the majority of the nine-member SC (Lords

Sumption, Clarke, Reed and Hughes J.S.C.C. dissenting) held that it would not have been outside the court's institutional power to declare the Suicide Act 1961 s.2 to be incompatible with the ECHR even though the question was one within the UK's margin of appreciation as far as the ECtHR was concerned. The majority stated that a declaration of incompatibility would not have the effect of forcing Parliament to act.

The content of Convention rights under the HRA

Absolute rights

The right to life

13–062 *[Delete all text in n.157 and substitute]*

In *Pretty v UK* (2002) 35 E.H.R.R. 1 at [38]–[40], the ECtHR followed the reasoning of the HL in rejecting a challenge by the victim of a degenerative disease to the Director of Public Prosecution's decision not to offer an assurance not to prosecute the victim's husband if he assisted her suicide. The HL decision is *R. (on the application of Pretty) v DPP* [2001] UKHL 61; [2002] 1 A.C. 800. The HL subsequently departed from its position in *Pretty* and required the Director of Public Prosecutions to clarify prosecution policy on assisted suicide on the grounds that the uncertainty in the current policy did not satisfy the requirements of art.8(2) (see *Purdy* at [54]–[56], n.86 above). The CPS published its new policy on assisted suicide in February 2010 (*http://www.cps.gov.uk/publications/prosecution/assisted_suicide_policy. html*). In *R. (on the application of Nicklinson) v Ministry of Justice* [2014] UKSC 38; [2014] 3 W.L.R. 200 at [141], [145], [249], [278], the SC declined to go further and tell the Director of Public Prosecutions what her policy should actually contain. The second reading of Lord Falconer's (private members') Assisted Dying Bill [HL] 2014–2015 took place on July 18, 2014.

[Add to end of n.158]

There is no requirement that there should be a risk to the life of an identified or identifiable individual; it is sufficient, for example, that individuals were known to be in the vicinity of the street where disorder was being caused (*Sarjantson v Chief Constable of Humberside Police* [2013] EWCA Civ 1252; [2014] Q.B. 411 at [22]–[36]).

13–063 *[Add to end of n.160]*

In *Smith v Ministry of Defence* [2013] UKSC 41; [2014] A.C. 41, the SC permitted claims of a breach of the positive substantive obligation in art.2 to proceed to trial. The claims related to the deaths of British servicemen in Iraq from improvised explosive devices while they were travelling in modified Land Rover vehicles.

[Add to end of n.163]   13–064

In *Keyu v Secretary of State for Foreign and Commonwealth Affairs* [2014] EWCA Civ 312 at [99]–[100], the CA held that the Inquiries Act 2005 (read with art.2) did not require the Secretary of State to establish a public inquiry into the Batang Kalir massacre in 1948 during the Malayan emergency as the CA continued to be bound by HL authority on retrospectivity of the HRA. In *R. (on the application of Litvinenko) v Secretary of State for the Home Department* [2013] EWHC 194 (Admin); [2014] H.R.L.R. 6 at [50]–[54], the DC found that the extensive police investigation into Mr Litvinenko's death was sufficient to fulfil art.2.

The right to be free from torture, inhuman and degrading treatment
or punishment

[In n.170 delete "Sentences of life . . . [25]–[30])" and substitute]   13–065

In *Vinter v UK* (App No.66069/09) (July 9, 2013) at [110]–[115], the ECtHR held that it was a breach of art.3 to impose whole life sentences on prisoners which only permitted release on compassionate grounds at the discretion of the Secretary of State. In *Re Attorney General's Reference (No.69 of 2013)* [2014] EWCA Crim 188; [2014] 3 All E.R. 73 at [25]–[36], a five-person CA held that, despite *Vinter,* such sentences were still permitted in exceptional cases and that the circumstances in which continued detention could be reviewed were sufficiently clear and had to be read consistently with art.3.

[Add to end of n.173]   13–066

If the conditions under which an asylum seeker would be required to live if returned to another state under the Dublin II Regulation (in this case Italy) created a real risk that art.3 would be violated (even if not as a result of systemic failings), this would violate the ECHR (*R. (on the application of EM (Eritrea)) v Secretary of State for the Home Department* [2014] UKSC 12; [2014] 2 W.L.R. 409 at [58]–[64], [68]–[69]). The case was remitted to the Administrative Court to determine on the facts whether such a risk arose.

[Add to end of n.176]

The relevant principles are summarised in *DSD v Commissioner of Police for the Metropolis* [2014] EWHC 436 (QB) at [211]–[225] in which the Administrative Court held that the police investigations relating to the so-called "Black cab rapist" did not fulfil art.3.

The prohibition on slavery and forced labour

13–068 *[Add to end of n.181]*

The SC in *Reilly* affirmed the CA's decision with regard to art.4: "Jobseeker's allowance, as its name suggests, is a benefit designed for a person seeking work, and the purpose of the condition is directly linked to the purpose of the benefit. The provision of a conditional benefit of that kind comes nowhere close to the type of exploitative conduct at which article 4 is aimed" ([2013] UKSC 68; [2014] A.C. 453 at [83]). The provisions were found to be ultra vires on other grounds. The claimant's art.4 submissions were not revisited in *R. (on the application of Reilly (No.2)) v Secretary of State for Work and Pensions* [2014] EWHC 2182 (Admin) which concerned the attempt to retrospectively validate the Regulations.

The ban on punishment without lawful authority

13–070 *[Add to end of n.189]*

Scoppola did not prevent a judge from imposing a sentence of imprisonment for public protection just before such sentences were abolished (see n.191) as life imprisonment was plainly a sentencing option in light of the nature of the offences (*R. v Docherty (Shaun Kevin)* [2014] EWCA Crim 1197 at [46]–[60]).

Limited rights

The right to liberty and security of the person

13–072 *[Add to end of n.191]*

In *R. (on the application of Sturnham) v Parole Board* [2013] UKSC 47; [2013] 2 A.C. 254 at [18]–[23], the SC confirmed that a breach of art.5(4) does not necessarily lead to a finding that art.5(1) has been violated, distinguishing *James*. A violation of art.5(1) will only follow if the detention has become arbitrary.

[Add to end of n.192]

The decision in *Hicks* was affirmed in the CA on modified grounds: [2014] EWCA Civ 3; [2014] 1 W.L.R. 2152 at [85]–[88] and required that those responsible for the arrest should have intended to bring the detainee before a competent legal authority at the time of the arrest even if this did not subsequently take place. On the inter-relation of art.5(1)(b) and (c), see *Ostendorf v Germany* (App. No.15598/08) (March 7, 2013) at [66]–[68], [82]–[86], [93]–[95] and the CA's criticisms of it in *Hicks*, above.

[Add to end of n.196]

See further, *Hassan v UK* (App.No.29750/09) (September 16, 2014).

[Add to end of n.197]   13–073

See *Mohammed v Ministry of Defence* [2014] EWHC 1369 (QB) (discussed at para.13–023).

[In n.198 delete final sentence and substitute]

In *Surrey County Council v P* [2014] UKSC 19; [2014] 2 W.L.R. 642 at [45]–[50], the majority of the SC held that a deprivation of liberty must be assessed objectively: living arrangements that would amount to a deprivation of liberty in the case of a non-disabled person would also be a deprivation of liberty in the case of a disabled person (irrespective of the reasons for the deprivation or whether the person consented). In *R. (on the application of Roberts) v Commissioner of Police of the Metropolis* [2014] EWCA Civ 69; [2014] 2 Cr. App. R. 6 at [10]–[13], the CA held that there was no deprivation of liberty under art.5 where the claimant was detained (at one point in handcuffs) in order for a police officer to search her under a stop and search authority granted under the Criminal Justice and Public Order Act 1994 s.60. Control orders were replaced with orders under the Terrorism Prevention and Investigation Measures Act 2011; on which, see *Mohamed v Secretary of State for the Home Department* [2014] EWCA Civ 559.

[Add to end of n.202]   13–075

In *R. (on the application of Osborn) v Parole Board* [2013] UKSC 61; [2013] 3 W.L.R. 1020 at [81]–[96], the SC indicated that an oral hearing before the Parole Board as a matter of common law fairness and compliance with art.5(4) was likely to be necessary where: important facts or issues of mitigation were in dispute; the Board could not otherwise make an independent assessment of risk; face-to-face encounter with the Board was necessary to enable the prisoner's case to be put or tested effectively; or where, in light of the prisoner's representations, it would be unfair for the matter to be determined on paper.

[Add to end of n.203]

In *Betteridge v UK* (2013) 57 E.H.R.R. 7, the ECtHR held that a delay in the applicant's Parole Board review breached art.5(4) and awarded €750 for non-pecuniary damage arising from feelings of frustration at the delay of just over a year.

The right to marry and found a family

13–078 *[Add to end of n.209]*

See further, *Vallianatos v Greece* (2014) 59 E.H.R.R. 12 (discussed at para.13–029).

Qualified rights

Necessary in a democratic society

13–084 *[Add to end of n.223]*

For a recent discussion of proportionality under the HRA, see *R. (on the application of MM (Lebanon)) v Secretary of State for the Home Department* [2014] EWCA Civ 985 at [139]–[153]. On proportionality more generally, see *Bank Mellat v HM Treasury (No.2)* [2013] UKSC 38; [2014] A.C. 700 at [20]–[21], [68]–[76], [93].

The right to respect for private and family life

13–085 *[In n.230 delete the final sentence and substitute]*

The Defamation Act 2013 came into force on April 25, 2013.

[Delete all text in n.231 and substitute]

Pretty v United Kingdom (2002) 35 E.H.R.R. 1 at [61]. A majority of the SC (Baroness Hale DPSC and Lord Kerr J.S.C. dissenting) rejected a challenge to the blanket ban on assisted suicide on the basis of art.8 in *R. (Nicklinson) v Ministry of Justice* [2014] UKSC 38; [2014] 3 W.L.R. 200.

13–086 *[Add to end of n.234]*

See *Vallianatos v Greece* (2014) 59 E.H.R.R. 12 on the ECtHR's developing recognition of same-sex relationships. In *R. (on the application of MM (Lebanon)) v Secretary of State for the Home Department* [2014] EWCA Civ 985 at [139]–[153], the CA rejected a challenge to the requirements of the Immigration Rules which imposed minimum income requirements on those with the right to live in the United Kingdom who wished to bring their spouses who were non-EEA citizens to this country.

[In n.236 delete final sentence and substitute]

In R. *(on the application of T) v Chief Constable of Greater Manchester Police* [2014] UKSC 35; [2014] 3 W.L.R. 96, the SC held that provisions in Pt V of the Police Act 1997 concerning the disclosure of enhanced criminal record certificates, including records of privately issued police cautions, constitute an aspect of the private life of the recipient and so engage art.8. The SC held that the provisions breached the requirements in art.8(2) since the cumulative effect of the failure to draw distinctions based on: the nature of the offence; the disposal of the case; the time elapsed since the offence took place; the relevance of the offence to the employment sought; and the absence of any independent review of the decision to disclose was that the provisions were not in accordance with the law (at [119], [158]). The SC also held that the provisions bore no rational connection to the assessment of the risks posed by those wishing to work with children or the elderly and were therefore not necessary in a democratic society (at [121], [158]). The DC held that the powers to detain and question those suspected of involvement in terrorism contained in Sch.7 to the Terrorism Act 2000 do not violate art.8 *(Beghal v Director of Public Prosecutions* [2013] EWHC 2573 (Admin); [2014] Q.B. 607 at [90]–[98], [105]–[112]).

[Add to end of n.237]

Norway's failure to provide information about the damaging effects of decompression on divers amounted to a breach of art.8 *(Vilnes v Norway* (App. No.52806/09) (December 5, 2013) at [233]–[245]).

[Add to end of n.239]   **13–087**

In *McDonald v UK* (App. No.4241/12) (May 20, 2014) at [53]–[58], the ECtHR found that the decision to reduce the amount allocated for Ms McDonald's care did interfere with her art.8 rights since it required her to wear incontinence pads at night when she was not incontinent and had previously been assisted to use the lavatory by a night-time carer. However, the ECtHR found the interference to be necessary in the field of allocating scarce welfare resources and to have appropriately balanced her needs against the interests of the wider community.

Freedom of thought, conscience and religion

[Add to end of n.242]   **13–088**

See further, J. Dingemans, C. Yeginsu, T. Cross and H. Masood, *The Protections for Religious Rights: Law and Practice* (2013).

[Add to end of n.243]

In *R. (on the application of Hodkin) v Registrar of Births, Deaths and Marriages* [2013] UKSC 77; [2014] A.C. 610, the SC held that a chapel of the Church of Scientology was a "place of meeting for religious worship" for the purposes of the Places of Worship Registration Act 1855.

13–089 *[Add to n.245 after "manifesting their religion"]*

The ECtHR found no violation of art.9 in *Church of Jesus Christ of Latter-Day Saints v UK* (2014) 59 E.H.R.R. 18.

[Add to n.246 after "Rafferty L.J.))"]

The SC affirmed the CA's decision in *Preddy v Bull* [2013] UKSC 73; [2013] 1 W.L.R. 3741 at [38]–[39] and [51]–[55]. For helpful discussion of the relationship between the state's duties under art.9 and art.11, see *Sindicatul "Păstorul Cel Bun" v Romania* (2014) 58 E.H.R.R. 10, discussed in the updated n.263 below.

[Add to end of n.246]

The CA upheld a requirement that a carer should work on Sundays despite her Christian faith since there was no other viable and practicable way of running a care home (*Mba v Merton LBC* [2013] EWCA Civ 1562; [2014] 1 W.L.R. 1501 at [34]–[37]).

Freedom of expression

13–090 *[Add to end of n.248]*

The ECtHR distinguished *Financial Times* and similar authorities in a case where the "source" in question was the perpetrator of a bomb attack whose disclosure was "not motivated by the desire to provide information which the public were entitled to know", but rather who "was claiming responsibility for crimes which he had himself committed . . . to don the veil of anonymity with a view to evading his own criminal accountability" (*Stichting Ostade Blade v Netherlands* (2014) 59 E.H.R.R. SE9 at [65]). Where the identity of the source is not secret, the issue does not arise as was the case with material appropriated by Edward Snowden: *Miranda v Secretary of State for the Home Department* [2014] EWHC 255 (Admin); [2014] H.R.L.R. 9 at [48]. In *Miranda*, the DC found that the stopping and detention of David Miranda at Heathrow airport for nine hours under Sch.7 of the Terrorism Act 2000 was proportionate, sufficiently certain in scope and subject to sufficient safeguards, such that it did not amount to a violation of his art.10 rights (at [72]–[73], [82]–[90]).

[Add to end of n.251]

In *R. (on the application of Core Issues Trust) v Transport for London* [2014] EWCA Civ 34; [2014] P.T.S.R. 785 at [63]–[70], [83]–[89], the CA upheld the defendant's decision to refuse to carry advertisements on its buses on behalf of a Christian organisation ("Not gay! Ex-gay, post-gay and proud. Get over it!"), which responded to a campaign that it had carried by Stonewall ("Some people are gay. Get over it."). Despite this preference for one viewpoint over another, the CA upheld the decision on the grounds that the Christian organisation's message may be offensive to homosexuals.

[In n.253 delete final sentence and substitute]

In *Kennedy v Charity Commission* [2014] UKSC 20; [2014] 2 W.L.R. 808 at [57]–[89], Lord Mance J.S.C. undertook an extensive review of the Strasbourg authorities concerning whether art.10 contained a positive right to receive information from the state. While acknowledging the ECtHR's apparent inconsistency on the point, the SC concluded that no such right could be said to exist on the present state of the authorities: [93]–[96], [144]–[148], [154]. See further, K. O'Byrne, "Freedom of Information under Article 10 ECHR and the Common Law" (2014) E.H.R.L.R. 284.

[Add to n.254 after ". . . [2009] P.L. 89"]

By the narrowest majority (of nine votes to eight), the ECtHR upheld the ban as proportionate on the basis of the widespread debate which preceded it and the impact of the broadcast media (*Animal Defenders International v UK* (2013) 57 E.H.R.R. 21 at [106]–[125]). See J. Rowbottom, "Animal Defenders International: Speech, Spending, and a Change of Direction in Strasbourg" (2013) 5 J.M.L. 1.

Freedom of peaceful assembly and association

[Add to n.262 after ". . . (Richards L.J.)"]   13–094

See now [2014] EWCA Civ 3; [2014] 1 W.L.R. 2152.

[Add to end of n.263]

The ECtHR held that a statutory ban on secondary industrial action did not breach art.11 in *National Union of Rail, Maritime and Transport Workers v UK* (App. No.31045/2010) (April 8, 2014) at [78]–[105]. In *Sindicatul "Păstorul Cel Bun" v Romania* (2014) 58 E.H.R.R. 10 at [143]–[145], [157], [159]–[173], the ECtHR held, by a majority of 11 to six, that a decision of a Romanian Court to revoke registration of a trade union comprised of members of the Orthodox clergy did not amount to a violation of art.11. While the duties performed by the clergy in question did have many of the characteristic features of an employment relationship (which had been denied by the Romanian Government), the ECtHR found that the decision was prescribed by law and not disproportionate (particularly in light of the state's duties under art.9 of the Convention).

The right to the enjoyment of possessions

13–096 *[Add to end of n.267]*

New London College Ltd was decided by the SC on other grounds: [2013] UKSC 51; [2013] 1 W.L.R. 2358. See further on this issue, *R. (on the application of Guildhall College) v Secretary of State for Business, Innovation and Skills* [2014] EWCA Civ 986 at [72]–[75]. *Salvesen v Riddell* [2013] UKSC 22 at [40]–[45] held that provisions of the Agricultural Holdings (Scotland) Act 2003 breached the art.1 rights of landlords. See further *Breyer Group Plc v Department of Energy and Climate Change* [2014] EWHC 2257 (QB) on the definition of possessions.

13–098 *[Add to end of n.274]*

Nor, when the state seeks to control the use of property, and could do so using different provisions with different consequences in terms of compensation, is there any requirement that it invoke the provision carrying some (or greater) compensation: *Cusack v Harrow LBC* [2013] UKSC 40; [2013] 1 W.L.R. 2022 at [45]–[49], [69].

The prohibition on discrimination

13–101 *[Add to end of n.283]*

Article 14 prohibits a third form of discrimination described in the case of *Thlimmenos v Greece* (2001) 31 E.H.R.R. 411 at [44]: where the state fails to treat differently persons whose situations are significantly distinct without objective and reasonable justification.

[Add to end of n.285]

The benefit cap introduced in the Welfare Reform Act 2012 was held to discriminate indirectly against women, but its discriminatory effect was not manifestly without reasonable foundation and so not unlawful: *R. (on the application of JS) v Secretary of State for Work and Pensions* [2014] EWCA Civ 156; [2014] P.T.S.R. 619 at [25]–[57]. The reduction in the eligible rent used to calculate housing benefit based on the number of bedrooms in the property discriminated against disabled people, but was justified in the circumstances (*R. (on the application of MA) v Secretary of State for Work and Pensions* [2014] EWCA Civ 13; [2014] P.T.S.R. 584 at [48]–[60]). On the other hand, it was a breach of art.14 read with art.6 (and the principle of equal treatment at common law) to seek to impose a residence requirement for legal aid cases in *R. (on the application of the Public Law Project) v Secretary of State for Justice* [2014] EWHC 2365 (Admin).

The impact of the HRA

[Add to n.290 after ". . . could be implemented"]   **13–104**

The Commission on a Bill of Rights appointed by the Coalition Government reported in two volumes in 2012: *A UK Bill of Rights? The Choice Before Us*. The majority of the Commission was in favour of a UK Bill of Rights in order to promote a sense of "ownership" by the public. The Commission expressed support for the inclusion in such a Bill of a right to equality and non-discrimination, perhaps with additional protections in the administrative and criminal justice fields. The majority opposed including socio-economic and environmental rights. The enforcement mechanisms would remain largely as under the HRA. The proposals are convincingly criticised by F. Klug and A. Williams, "The Choice Before Us? The Report of the Commission on a Bill of Rights" [2013] P.L. 459.

[Delete existing heading of Table 1 and substitute]

Table 1: Declarations of incompatibility under HRA s.4—updated to September 2014

[Add to end of Table 1]

	Judgment	Right	Legislation	Response
20	*R (on the application of Reilly (No. 2)) v Secretary of State for Work and Pensions* [2014] EWHC 2182 (Admin)	Art.6.1	Jobseekers (Back to Work Schemes) Act 2013; retroactive effect not justified by compelling grounds of the general interest	The Secretary of State has been granted permission to appeal. No remedial action has been taken
21	*R. (on the application of T) v Chief Constable of Greater Manchester Police* [2014] UKSC 35; [2014] 3 W.L.R. 96	Art.8	Police Act 1997	Repealed by the Serious Organised Crime and Police Act 2005

CHAPTER 14

REVIEW UNDER EUROPEAN UNION LAW

INTRODUCTON

[In n.11 delete "10th edn (2012)" and substitute]   **14–002**

11th edn (2014)

[In n.11 delete "7th edn (2010)" and substitute]

8th edn (2014)

OVERVIEW OF THE EU LEGAL SYSTEM

[Add new n.22a after "... enhanced cooperation"]   **14–005**

22a For recent consideration, see *Spain and Italy v Council* (Cases C-274/11 and C-295/11) (April 16, 2013).

Policy areas within the field of the European Union

[In para.14–010 delete "or decentralised"]   **14–010**

[In n.33 delete "Regulation (EC) 1605/2002 on the Financial Regulation Applicable to the General Budget of the European Communities [2002] OJ L248/1 art 53(b)" and substitute]

Regulation (EU, Euratom) No 966/2012 of the European Parliament and of the Council of October 25, 2012 on the financial rules applicable to the general budget of the Union and repealing Council Regulation (EC, Euratom) No 1605/2002 art.58(1)(b);

[In para.14–010 delete "'centralised' management" and substitute]

"direct" or "indirect" management

[In n.34 delete "Regulation (EC) 1605/2002 on the Financial Regulation Applicable to the General Budget of the European Communities [2002] OJ L248/1 arts 53(a), 53a, and 54–57" and substitute]

Regulation (EU, EURATOM) 966/2012 on the financial rules applicable to the general budget of the Union and repealing Council Regulation (EC, Euratom) No 1605/2002 [2012] OJ L298/1 arts 58(1)(a), 58(1)(b), 60–63.

[Add to end of n.35]

For recent consideration of competence by the ECJ, see *Commission v Council* (C-137/12) (October 22, 2013); *Daiichi Sankyo and Sanofi-Aventis Deutschland* (C-414/11) (July 18, 2013); and *United Kingdom v Council* (C-431/11) (First Chamber, September 26, 2013).

Primacy of Union law

14–012   *[Add new para.14–012A after para.14–012]*

14–012A There may, however, be limits to the primacy of EU law. In *R. on the application of Buckinghamshire v Secretary of State for Transport*.[42a] In this case, requirements laid down in Directive 2011/92/EU concerning the way in which Member States take certain decisions were at issue, including the decision in respect of the construction of the proposed "HS2" high-speed rail network. The decision was taken through the enactment of a "hybrid Bill", which was described as effectively a public bill, which affects a particular private interest in a manner different from the private interests of other persons or bodies of the same category or class.[42b] The difficulty with scrutinising the decision-making process therefore was that it might impinge "upon long-established constitutional principles governing the relationship between Parliament and the courts, as reflected for example in article 9 of the Bill of Rights 1689".[42c] It was decided that the Directive did not require review that was constitutionally problematic, but considered briefly what would have happened had the Directive called for such scrutiny and commented as follows:

> "resolved simply by applying the doctrine developed by the Court of Justice of the supremacy of EU law, since the application of that doctrine in our law itself depends upon the [European Communities Act 1972]. If there is a conflict between a constitutional principle, such as that embodied in article 9 of the Bill of Rights, and EU law, that conflict has to be resolved by our courts as an issue arising under the constitutional law of the United Kingdom. Nor can the issue be resolved, as was also suggested, by following the decision in *R v Secretary of State for Transport, Ex p Factortame Ltd (No 2)* [1991] 1 AC 603, since that case was not concerned with the compatibility with EU law of the process by which legislation is enacted in Parliament."[42d]

[42a] [2014] UKSC 3; [2014] 1 W.L.R. 324.

[42b] [2014] UKSC 3; [2014] 1 W.L.R. 324 at [57].

[42c] [2014] UKSC 3; [2014] 1 W.L.R. 324 at [78].

[42d] [2014] UKSC 3; [2014] 1 W.L.R. 324 at [79].

Direct effect of Union law measures

[Add to end of n.44]   **14–013**

; *Association de médiation sociale v Union locale des syndicats CGT* (C-176/12) (Grand Chamber, January 15, 2014) at [31].

[Add to end of n.47]

; *Association de médiation sociale v Union locale des syndicats CGT* (C-176/12) (Grand Chamber, January 15, 2014) at [44]–[45] (Charter art.27 must be given more specific expression in European Union or national law).

[Add to n.51 after ". . . I-5939 at [41]–[46]"]

; *Fra.bo Spa v Deutsche Vereinigung des Gas-und Wasserfaches eV* (C-171/11) (July 12, 2012) at [31]–[32] (holding that TFEU art.34 applied to a private standardisation and certification body where the body "in reality [held] the power to regulate the entry into the German market of products such as the copper fittings at issue in the main proceedings").

SECONDARY LEGISLATION

Directives

Direct Effect of Directives

[Add to end of n.71]   **14–022**

; *Association de médiation sociale v Union locale des syndicats CGT* (C-176/12) (Grand Chamber, January 15, 2014) at [36].

[Add to end of n.83]   **14–024**

See also *Fish Legal v Information Commissioner* (C-279/12) [2014] Q.B. 521 at [64]–[73] (in the context of art.2 of Directive 2003/4/EC of the

113

European Parliament and of the Council of January 28, 2003 on public access to environmental information and repealing Council Directive 90/313/EEC, to determine whether an entity is a legal person which performs "public administrative functions", it is necessary to examine whether those entities are vested, under national law, with special powers beyond those which result from the normal rules applicable in relations between persons governed by private law and a body will be under the "control" of such an entity where it does not determine in a genuinely autonomous manner the way in which it provides those services since a public authority is in a position to exert decisive influence on its action in the environmental field).

THE CHARTER OF FUNDAMENTAL RIGHTS OF THE EU

14–030 *[Add to end of n.103]*

; K. O'Brien and B. Kolterman, "The Charter of Fundamental Rights of the EU in Practice" (2013) 14 ERA Forum 457.

[Add to end of n.112]

See also *R. (on the application of AB) v Secretary of State for the Home Department* [2013] EWHC 3453 (Admin); [2014] 2 C.M.L.R. 22 at [12]–[16] (obiter, noting that the Charter "enunciates a host of new rights" not expressly incorporated into EU law under the Human Rights Act 1998).

[Add to end of n.114]

The distinction between rights and principles may have an impact on whether a Charter provision may have horizontal direct effect: *Association de médiation sociale v Union locale des syndicats CGT* (C-176/12) (Opinion of AG Villalón) [2014] I.C.R. 411 at [49]–[60] (differing from the Advocate General and considering that rights may have such effects, but principles may not); and (C-176/12) (Grand Chamber, January 15, 2014) at [43]–[48] (finding that some Charter provisions, such as art.21(1), are capable of horizontal direct effect, but others, such as art.27, are not). See also N. Lazzerini, "(Some of) the Fundamental Rights Granted by the Charter may be a Source of Obligations for Private Parties" [2014] 51(3) C.M.L. Rev. 907; H. Hofmann and B. Mihaescu, "The Relation between the Charter's Fundamental Rights and the Unwritten General Principles of EU Law: Good Administration as the Test Case" [2013] 9(1) E.C.L. Review 73.

[Add to end of n.117]

; cf. *R. (on the application of EM (Eritrea)) v Secretary of State for the Home Department* [2014] UKSC 12; [2014] 2 W.L.R. 409 at [44]–[62] (the

Supreme Court, when faced with an ECJ interpretation of a Charter right which would involve incompatibility with ECHR art.3, considered that the ECJ "did not intend" to alter the meaning of art.3).

[In n.119 delete "(art.53) does not mean national rights override EU law)" and substitute]

[60] (holding that, while art.53 confirms that national courts remain free to apply national standards of protection of fundamental rights, this is "provided that the level of protection provided for by the Charter, as interpreted by the Court, and the primacy, unity and effectiveness of EU law are not thereby compromised"). On the facts of the case, this meant that the Spanish courts could not make the surrender, pursuant to Framework Decision 2002/584, of a person convicted in absentia conditional upon the conviction being open to review in the issuing Member State, in order to avoid an adverse effect on the right to a fair trial and the rights of defence guaranteed by the national constitution: [64]. The Spanish Constitutional Court reacted by lowering the degree of protection afforded by the Spanish Constitution in line with Union law: STC 26/2014. See also *Cruciano Siragusa v Regione Sicilia – Soprintendenza Beni Culturali e Ambientali di Palermo* (C-206/13) (March 6, 2014) at [32]. For discussion of *Melloni*, see, eg A. Torres Perez, "*Melloni* in Three Acts: From Dialogue to Monologue" (2014) 10 E.C.L. Review 308; L.F.M. Besselink, "The Parameters of Constitutional Conflict after *Melloni*" (2014) 39 E.L. Rev. 531.

[Add to end of n.125]   14–031

See also *Digital Rights Ireland v Minister for Communications, Marine and Natural Resources* (C-293, 594/12) (Grand Chamber, April 8, 2014) at [45]–[70] (holding that the Data Retention Directive violated art.7 of the Charter due to a lack of proportionality); *Google Inc v Agencia Española de Protección de Datos (AEPD)* (C-131/12) (Grand Chamber, May 13, 2014) at [97]–[99] (finding that the right to private life and the production of personal data overrode the economic interests of the operator of a search engine and the interests of the general public, unless the data in question played a role in public life).

[Add to para.14–031 after ". . . novel aspects of the Charter, such as"]

workers' rights to information and consultation in art.27,[126a]

[126a] *Association de médiation sociale v Union locale des syndicats CGT* (C-176/12) (Grand Chamber, January 15, 2014).

[Add to end of n.128]

115

; *Užsienio reikalų ministerija v Vladimir Peftiev* (C-314/13) (June 12, 2014) (freezing of funds should not prevent access to legal representation); *Inuit Tapiriit Kanatami v Parliament and Council* (C-583/11) [2014] Q.B. 648; [2014] 1 C.M.L.R. 54 at [105] (art.47 does not require that an individual should have an unconditional entitlement to bring an action for annulment of Union legislative acts directly before the courts of the European Union); *Commission v Kadi (Bulgaria intervening)* (C-584/10P, C-593/10P, C-595/10P) (Grand Chamber) [2014] 1 C.M.L.R. 24; *ZZ v Secretary of State for the Home Department* (C-300/11) (June 4, 2013) at [57] (where a national authority opposes disclosure of documents submitted to a court for reasons of state security, the court with jurisdiction in the Member State concerned must have at its disposal and apply techniques and rules of procedural law which accommodate, on the one hand, legitimate State security considerations and on the other hand, the need to ensure sufficient compliance with the person's procedural rights); *R. (on the application of Edwards and Pallikaropoulos) v Environment Agency* (C-260/11) (April 11, 2013) at [35] (the requirement in art.10a of Council Directive 85/337/EEC of 27 June 1985 on the assessment of the effects of certain public and private projects on the environment [1985] OJ L175/40 meant that proceedings should not be prohibitively expensive means that persons concerned should not be prevented from seeking, or pursuing a claim for, a review by the courts that falls within the scope of the relevant provisions of EU law by reason of the financial burden that might arise as a result). See also *Commission v United Kingdom of Great Britain and Northern Ireland* (C-530/11) (February 13, 2014).

[Add after ". . . of art.47"]

; see also *Schindler Holding v Commission* (C-501/11) (July 18, 2013) at [33]–[34].

14–032 *[Add new para.14–032A after para.14–032]*

14–032A Following *Åklagaren*, the ECJ has also explained, in *Cruciano Siragusa*, that the concept of "implementing Union law" requires a certain degree of connection with Union law above and beyond the matters covered being closely related or one of those matters having an indirect impact on the other. When determining whether national legislation involves the implementation of Union law, some of the points to be considered are whether that legislation is intended to implement a provision of Union law; the nature of that legislation and whether it pursues objectives other than those covered by Union law, even if it is capable of indirectly affecting Union law; and also whether there are specific rules of EU law on the matter or capable of affecting it. Furthermore, the fact that national legislation could have an indirect effect on a system established by Union law could not constitute a sufficient connection to bring such legislation within the scope of Union law. This meant that an order requiring a property owner to restore property within a landscape conservation area to its original state did not engage art.17 of the Charter where EU law did not impose any obligations to protect the specific landscape; there was only an indirect connection between the facts and Union law which was not sufficient to attract the application of the Charter.[138a]

[138a] *Cruciano Siragusa v Region Sicilia – Soprintendenza Beni Culturali e Ambientali di Palermo* (C-206/13) (March 6, 2014) at [24]–[27]. The ECJ also observed (at [22]) that Member States were only bound by EU funda-mental rights in respect of matters "covered by EU law". See also *Érsekcsanádi Mezogazdasági Zrt v Bács-Kiskun Megyei Kormányhivatal* (C-56/13) (May 22, 2014) (parts of a national implementing measure providing for compen-sation to affected parties could not be challenged under the Charter because the compensation provisions themselves were not part of the original direc-tive; this was so despite the fact that the national measure implemented EU law, and that the court had previously held that the EU may consider full or partial compensation for owners of farms whose animals have been destroyed); *Pelckmans Turnhout NV v Walter Van Gastel Balen NV* (C-483/12) (May 8, 2014) at [20] (prohibition on seven-day trading outside the scope of Union law and could not be considered for compatibility with the Charter).

[Add new para.14–032B after 14–032A]

It has been held that certain provisions of the Charter are capable of hori-zontal direct effect, although there is a lack of clarity on which provisions are capable of such effect.[138b] **14–032B**

[138b] *Association de médiation sociale v Union locale des syndicats CGT* (C-176/12) (Grand Chamber, January 15, 2014) at [43]–[48].

[Add to end of n.139] **14–033**

See *Digital Rights Ireland v Minister for Communications, Marine and Natural Resources* (C-293, 594/12) (Grand Chamber, April 8, 2014) at [45]–[71] for an example of a case in which legislation, the Data Retention Directive, was found incompatible with the Charter due to a lack of proportionality.

[Add to end of para.14–034] **14–034**

The ECJ's approach was considered in *R. (on the application of AB) v Secretary of State for the Home Department* by Mostyn J., who regarded it as "absolutely clear that the contracting parties agreed that the Charter did not create one single further justiciable right in our domestic courts" but that this view was not shared by the ECJ.[141a] The Supreme Court has also observed recently that the UK, as an EU Member State, is obliged to observe and promote the application of the Charter whenever implementing an instrument of EU law.[141b]

[141a] [2013] EWHC 3453 (Admin); [2014] 2 C.M.L.R. 22 at [12]–[13].

[141b] *R. (on the application of EM (Eritrea)) v Secretary of State for the Home Department* [2014] UKSC 12; [2014] 2 W.L.R. 409 at [62].

GENERAL PRINCIPLES OF LAW

14–035 *[Add new n.143a after ". . . [ex EC art.288(2)]."]*

[143a] See, e.g. *Commission v Systran and Systran Luxembourg* (C-103/11) (First Chamber, April 18, 2013).

[Add to n.146 after ". . . was reaffirmed in Kücükdeveci"]

Likewise, in *Association de médiation sociale v Union locale des syndicats CGT* (C-176/12) (January 15, 2014) at [41], the ECJ endorsed *Kücükdeveci*, albeit in passing and albeit distinguishing it from the circumstances at issue.

[Add to end of n.146]

; C. Murphy, "Using the EU Charter of Fundamental Rights against Private Parties after Association de Mediation Sociale" [2014] E.H.R.L.R. 170.

EUROPEAN COMMUNITES ACT 1972 AND THE EUROPEAN UNION ACT 2011

14–036 *[Add to end of n.147]*

; *R. (on the application of Buckinghamshire County Council) v Secretary of State for Transport* [2014] UKSC 3; [2014] P.T.S.R. 182 at [207] (describing it as a "constitutional instrument").

14–041 *[Add to end of n.160]*

; S. Peers, "European Integration and the European Union Act 2011: An Irresistible Force Meets an Immovable Object" [2013] P.L. 119.

INTERPRETATION BY NATIONAL COURTS

[Add to end of n.185]　　　　　　　　　　　　　　　　　　　　14–048

For a useful discussion of the use of recitals in interpretation of EU secondary legislation, see *Recall Support Services Ltd v Secretary of State for Culture, Media and Sport* [2013] EWHC 3091 (Ch); [2014] 2 C.M.L.R. 2 at [50].

[Add to end of n.187]

The ECJ has recently explained that a provision of Union law itself will be interpreted in light of its wording and objectives, its context and the provisions of Union law as a whole, as well as its origins: *Inuit Tapiriit Kanatami v Parliament and Council* (Case C-583/11) [2014] Q.B. 648; [2014] 1 C.M.L.R. 54 at [50]. In this case, the ECJ placed particular emphasis on the *travaux préparatoires*: [59], [60], [70].

[In para.14–051 delete "in the past"]　　　　　　　　　　　　　14–051

[Add to end of n.201]

Association de médiation sociale v Union locale des syndicats CGT (C-176/12) (January 15, 2014) at [39].

[Add to end of n.205]　　　　　　　　　　　　　　　　　　　　14–052

; *Association de médiation sociale v Union locale des syndicats CGT* (C-176/12) (Grand Chamber, January 15, 2014) at [39].

[Add to end of n.206]

; *Prudential Assurance Co. Ltd. v Revenue and Customs Commissioners* [2013] EWHC 3249 (Ch); [2014] 2 C.M.L.R 10 at [102], [105] (*Marleasing* implies a "highly muscular" approach to conforming interpretation).

EFFECTIVE PROCEDURES AND REMEDIES

Principle of effective judicial protection

[In n.223 delete "Commission Draft Guidance Paper on quantifying harm in 　14–057
actions for damages based on breaches of the EU antitrust rules (2011), available at http://ec.europa.eu/competition/consultations/2011_actions_damages/ draft_guidance_paper_en.pdf (accessed March 25, 2013)" and substitute]

119

Communication from the Commission on quantifying harm in actions for damages based on breaches of Article 101 or 102 [TFEU] [2012] OJ C167/07.

Limitation Periods

14–066 *[Add to n.271 after ". . . Levez [1998] ECR I-7835 at [20], [27]–[34]"]*

See also *Birmingham Hippodrome Theatre Trust Ltd v Commissioners for HM Revenue and Customs* [2014] EWCA Civ 684; [2014] B.V.C. 27 at [46]–[49] (noting that "certainty is not a trump card" such that it did not breach the principles of effectiveness, equality or legal certainty for Revenue and Customs to be entitled to set off a repayment of input tax which should not have been made against a taxpayer's claim for repayment of output tax, despite being out of time to claim repayment of the wrongly repaid input tax).

State liability in damages for breach of Union law

14–075 *[Add new n.304a after ". . . for which they are held responsible"]*

[304a] The High Court has recently affirmed that a person adversely affected by a breach of EU law is not required to challenge the legality of the measure in proceedings before the national court before bringing a claim for *Francovich* damages: see *Recall Support Services Ltd v Secretary of State for Culture, Media and Sport* [2013] EWHC 3091 (Ch); [2014] 2 C.M.L.R. 2 at [220] (following *Metallgesellschaft Ltd v Inland Revenue Commissioners* (C-397/98) [2001] E.C.R. I-1727).

Sufficiently serious breach

14–078 *[Add to end of n.322]*

; *Recall Support Services Ltd v Secretary of State for Culture, Media and Sport* [2013] EWHC 3091 (Ch); [2014] 2 C.M.L.R. 2 at [165].

[Add to end of n.323]

; *Specht v Land Berlin* (C-501/12-C-506/12) (June 19, 2014) at [105] (legislation which is not clear and precise may become so from the date upon which the court gives clarity and definition to a rule of EU law).

[Add to end of n.330]

Hogan v Minister for Social and Family Affairs (C-398/11) [2013] 3 C.M.L.R. 27 at [51]–[52] (the requirements of art.8 of Directive 80/987 as amended were clear and specific from the date of a prior judgment, as such, Ireland's failure to transpose the Directive correctly gave rise to a sufficiently serious breach of Union law); *Specht v Land Berlin* (C-501/12-C-506/12) (June 19, 2014) at [105] (legislation which is not clear and precise may become so from the date upon which the court gives clarity and definition to a rule of EU law).

PRELIMINARY RULINGS

Limitations to the jurisdiction of the court in a preliminary reference

[Add to end of n.366]   14–088

; see also *Érsekcsanádi Mezogazdasági Zrt v Bács-Kiskun Megyei Kormányhivatal* (C-56/13) (May 22, 2014) at [48]–[57] (a national requirement to pay compensation subject to an exclusion of compensation for loss of profits in an implementing measure where the EU measure did not provide for any compensation could not be challenged under the Charter and the ECJ did not have jurisdiction to rule on it).

The referral discretion of the lower courts

[Add to end of n.374]   14–089

The ECJ has also emphasised recently that a national procedural rule pursuant to which legal rulings of a higher court bind the lower courts cannot call into question the discretion of the latter courts to request the court for a preliminary ruling where they have doubts as to the interpretation of European Union law: *Križan v Slovenská inšpekcia životného prostredia* (C-416/10) (January 15, 2013) at [67].

[Add to end of n.377]

For a recent summary of the position, see *Fish Legal v Information Commissioner* (C-279/12) (Grand Chamber, December 19, 2013) at [30].

[Add to end of n.378]

; *Fish Legal v Information Commissioner* (C-279/12) (Grand Chamber, December 19, 2013) at [30]; *Maatschap T van Oosterom en A van Oosterom-Boelhouwer v Staatssecretaris van Economische Zaken* (C-485/12) (April 10, 2014) at [31]–[32] (presumption cannot be rebutted by fact that the facts remain contested).

[Add to end of n.384]

121

; *Revenue and Customs Commissioners v Aimia Coalition Loyalty UK Ltd* [2013] UKSC 15; [2013] 2 C.M.L.R. 51 (declining to follow the ECJ's ruling in a preliminary reference, or make a further preliminary reference, where the ECJ had ruled on arguments not made by the parties, and due to the UK court's understanding of the established EU principle and greater understanding of the facts and arguments made).

[Add to end of n.389]

There has been some gentle criticism of the ECJ by the Supreme Court recently. In *Revenue and Customs Commissioners v Aimia Coalition Loyalty UK Ltd* [2013] UKSC 15; [2013] 2 C.M.L.R. 51 at [87], Lord Hope observed that a judgment, in respect of which the ECJ had not sought an opinion from the Advocate General before it proceeded to judgment, lacked the depth of reasoning which a judgment informed by an opinion would have provided, albeit that his Lordship noted that this was quite rare.

Referral obligation of national courts of last instance

14–090 *[Add to end of n.390]*

See also *Križan v Slovenská inšpekcia životného prostredia* (C-416/10) (January 15, 2013) at [62] (the ECJ ruling that a national court is a court against whose decisions there is no judicial remedy under national law, within the meaning of TFEU art.267(3) and which is thus required to request a preliminary ruling, even where national law provides for the possibility of bringing before the constitutional court of the Member State concerned an action against is decisions limited to an examination of a potential infringement of the rights and freedoms guaranteed by the national constitution or by an international agreement).

[Add to end of n.393]

; *R. (on the application of Buckinghamshire County Council) v Secretary of State for Transport* [2014] UKSC 3; [2014] P.T.S.R. 182 at [53], [117], [128]; *Revenue and Customs Commissioners v Aimia Coalition Loyalty UK Ltd* [2013] UKSC 15; [2013] 2 C.M.L.R. 51.

DIRECT ACTIONS IN THE ECJ AND GENERAL COURT

Enforcement

14–093 *[Add to end of n.406]*

For a recent example, see *Commission v Germany* (C-95/12) (October 22, 2013) (dismissal of an action brought by the Commission for a failure to comply with a previous judgment of the ECJ finding a failure to fulfil obligations).

Review of legality

For recent examples of annulment actions, see *Inuit Tapiriit Kanatami v Parliament and Council* (C-583/11) ([2014] Q.B. 648) and *Telefónica v Commission* (C-274/12 P) (December 19, 2013). **14–094**

[Add to end of n.412] **14–096**

; A. Kornezov, "Locus standi of Private Parties in Actions for Annulment: Has the Gap been Closed?" [2014] 73(1) C.L.J. 25.

[Add to end of n.414]

It was held in *Telefónica v Commission* (C-274/12 P) (December 19, 2013) at [30]–[31] that the question of whether a regulatory act entails "implementing measures" must be assessed by reference to the position of the person pleading the right to bring proceedings and that it is irrelevant whether the act in question entails implementing measures with regard to other persons. Furthermore, reference should be made exclusively to the subject matter of the action, and where the applicant seeks only the partial annulment of an act, it is solely the implementing measures which that part of the act entails that must, as the case may be, be taken into consideration.

[Delete "It is not yet clear to what extent the ECJ's approach will change in light of the revised test." and substitute] **14–097**

The impact of the revised test has been explored recently.

[Add to start of n.415]

Inuit Tapiriit Kanatami v Parliament and Council (Case C-583/11) [2014] Q.B. 648; [2014] 1 C.M.L.R. 54; *Telefónica v Commission* (C-274/12 P) (December 19, 2013).

[Add to end of n.417]

and (Grand Chamber) [2014] Q.B. 648; [2014] 1 C.M.L.R. 54 at [59].

[Add to para.14–097 after ". . .direct and individual concern.[417]"]

This position has been endorsed by the ECJ which has accepted that the term "regulatory act" does not extend to legislative acts.[417a]

[417a] *Inuit Tapiriit Kanatami v Parliament and Council* (C-583/11) [2014] Q.B. 648; [2014] 1 C.M.L.R. 54 at [60]. The ECJ rejected an argument made in the case for the requirement for "direct and individual concern" to be replaced with a criterion of "substantial adverse effect": [69]–[71]. The case is also notable for its heavy reliance on the *travaux preparatoires* relating to Article III-365(4) of the proposed Treaty establishing a Constitution for Europe, the content of which was reproduced in identical terms in TFEU art.263(4).

14–099 *[In n.421 delete "(pending appeal: C-267/11)" and substitute]*

(the point was not raised on appeal: C-267/11 P (October 3, 2013) at [46]).

[Add to end of n.422]

; *Commission v Kadi (Bulgaria intervening)* (C-584/10P, C-593/10P, C-595/10P) (Grand Chamber) [2014] 1 C.M.L.R. 24 at [134].

[Add to end of n.423]

See, e.g. *Commission v Kadi* [2014] 1 C.M.L.R. 24 at [130] (finding that if the application of a contested asset-freezing measure has grounding in at least one valid reason, the decision will not be annulled, notwithstanding that the same cannot be said of other reasons).

GROUNDS FOR JUDICIAL REVIEW AGAINST UNION MEASURES: OVERVIEW

14–100 *[Add to end of n.428]*

; *Commission v Kadi* [2014] 1 C.M.L.R. 24 at [97].

Proportionality

14–105 *[Add to n.447 after ". . . and third test': p.139"]*

More recently, in *Herbert Schaible v Land Baden-Württemberg* (C-101/12), Advocate General Wahl (May 29, 2013) expressed the view at [40] that the court's jurisdiction also extends to evaluating whether the measure strikes a fair balance between the interests of those affected, i.e. proportionality *stricto sensu*).

[Add to end of n.447]

; *Herbert Schaible v Land Baden-Württemberg* (C-101/12) at [29]; *Digital Rights Ireland v Minister for Communications, Marine and Natural Resources* (C-293, 594/12) (Grand Chamber, April 8, 2014) at [45]–[70].

Human rights

[Add to end of n.511] 14–116

See now *Gascogne Sack Deutschland GmbH v Commission* (C-40/12); *Kendrion NV v Commission* (C-50/12); *Groupe Gascogne SA v Commission* (C-58/12) (November 26, 2014).

[Add to end of n.512]

; *Inuit Tapiriit Kanatami v Parliament and Council* (C-583/11) [2014] Q.B. 648; [2014] 1 C.M.L.R. 54 at [105] (art.47 does not require that an individual should have an unconditional entitlement to bring an action for annulment of Union legislative acts directly before the Courts of the European Union); *Abdulraihim v Council of the European Union and European Commission* (C-239/12 P) (Grand Chamber) [2013] 3 C.M.L.R. 41 at [67]–[70] (effective judicial protection meant that an appellant still had an interest in annulling legislation which had already been repealed, since annulment was retrospective and not merely *ex nunc*).

[Add to para.14–116 after "... freedom of trade[518]"]

, freedom to conduct business.[518a]

[518a] See, e.g. *Herbert Schaible v Land Baden-Württemberg* (C-101/12) (October 17, 2013).

Emerging principles

[Add to end of n.535] 14–118

In the environmental context, see *Križan v Slovenská inšpekcia životného prostredia* (C-416/10) (January 15, 2013).

[Add to end of n.542]

In *Recall Support Services Ltd v Secretary of State for Culture, Media and Sport* [2013] EWHC 3091 (Ch); [2014] 2 C.M.L.R. 2, the principle was described (at [112]) as meaning that a Member State did not have to wait until some harm arose to the public before adopting measures to prevent a recurrence of that harm and which required authorities to take appropriate measures to prevent potential risks to public health, safety and the environment, by giving precedence to the requirements related to the protection of those interests over economic interests. Whether to have recourse to the precautionary principle depends on the level of protection chosen by the competent authority in the exercise of its discretion, taking account of the priorities that it defined in the light of the objectives it pursued in accordance with the relevant rules of the Treaty and of secondary law.

The requirement to state reasons

14–120 *[Add to para.14–120 after ". . .exercise its power of review.*[546]*"]*

Where provision of the reasons preclude the disclosure to the person concerned of information or evidence produced before the courts of the European Union due to security concerns, it is necessary to strike an appropriate balance between the requirements attached to the right to effective judicial protection and those flowing from the security of the Union or its Member States or the conduct of their international relations.[546a]

[546a] *Commission v Kadi* (C-584/10) [2014] 1 C.M.L.R. 24 at [128].

[Add to end of n.546]

; *Commission v Kadi* (C-584/10) [2014] 1 C.M.L.R. 24 at [116] (for the requirements for reasons where the reasons represent reasons stated by an international body where the Union is implementing international measures).

14–121 *[Add to end of n.553]*

The reasoning may be "implicit, on condition it enables the persons concerned to know why the measures in question were taken and provides the competent court with sufficient material for it to exercise its power of review": *Inuit Tapiriit Kanatami v Parliament and Council* (C-583/11) [2014] Q.B. 648; [2014] 1 C.M.L.R. 54 at [82].

14–124 *[Add to end of n.563]*

; *Commission v Kadi* [2014] 1 C.M.L.R. 24 at [116]–[117].

GROUNDS FOR JUDICIAL REVIEW OF NATIONAL MEASURES

[Add to end of n.571]   **14–126**

Recall Support Services Ltd v Secretary of State for Culture, Media and Sport
[2013] EWHC 3091 (Ch); [2014] 2 C.M.L.R. 2; *R. (on the application of*
Buckinghamshire CC) v Secretary of State for Transport [2014] UKSC 3;
[2014] 1 W.L.R. 324 (unsuccessful challenge to a Government Command
Paper setting out parameters for a high speed rail project).

The requirement to state reasons

[Add to end of n.581]   **14–130**

; *Commission v Kadi* [2014] 1 C.M.L.R. 24 at [111].

Fundamental rights

Where the Member State is not directly implementing EU measures

[Add to end of n.594]   **14–137**

For recent parallel developments in the context of the Charter, see
para.14–032A.

Part III
PROCEDURES AND REMEDIES

CHAPTER 15

THE HISTORICAL DEVELOPMENT OF JUDICIAL REVIEW REMEDIES AND PROCEDURES

There is no update to this historical account.

CHAPTER 16

CPR PT 54 CLAIMS FOR JUDICIAL REVIEW

SCOPE

[Add to n.9 after "31"]   16–002

, 31A

[Add to end of n.9]

The Government's proposals for extensive reforms to the judicial review procedure are described at paras 1–005 and 1–005A.

[In n.11 delete final two sentences and substitute]

Section 6(4) of the Justice and Security Act 2013 (which came into force on June 25, 2013) sets out the conditions under which the court (on the application of either of the parties or the Secretary of State, or of its own motion) may declare that a closed material application may be made; see para.8–009. The Bill which led to the 2013 Act was convincingly criticised by A. Peto and A. Tyrie, *Neither Just nor Secure* (2012).

[In n.12 delete "May 2012" and substitute]

August 2014

[In n.13 delete "http://www.justice.gov.uk/downloads/courts/administrative-court" and substitute]

http://www.justice.gov.uk/courts/rcj-rolls-building/administrative-court/applying-for-judicial-review.

THE ADMINISTRATIVE COURT

[Delete sentence "The following considerations are relevant to determining   16–003
the appropriate venue for proceedings:" and substitute]

The general expectation is that proceedings will be administered and determined in the region with which the claimant has the closest connection, subject to the following considerations:

[Add to para.16–003 after ". . . media interest in a particular area;"]

the time within which it is appropriate for the proceedings to be determined;

16–012 *[Add to end of n.42]*

See also *San Vicente v Secretary of State for Communities and Local Government* [2013] EWCA Civ 817; [2014] 1 W.L.R. 966 at [52] on applications to amend claims under s.288 of the Town and Country Planning Act 1990. In relation to applying the new provisions on relief from sanctions in CPR r.3.9, see *Mitchell v News Group Newspapers Ltd* [2013] EWCA Civ 1537; [2014] 1 W.L.R. 795 at [40]–[41] and *Denton v TH White Ltd* [2014] EWCA Civ 906 at [24]–[38]. In *Denton*, the CA set out the three stages which should be addressed: to identify and assess the seriousness and significance of the failure to comply with any rule, practice direction or court order; then to consider why the default occurred; and finally to evaluate all the circumstances of the case in order to deal with the application justly.

THE PROCEDURAL STAGES

Exhaustion of other remedies and ADR

16–014 *[In n.45 delete "(May 2012)" and substitute]*

(August 2014)

[Add to end of n.45]

See also *R. (on the application of Willford) v Financial Services Authority* [2013] EWCA Civ 677 at [36]–[38] (Upper Tribunal "can reconsider the whole matter afresh" and therefore provides a more appropriate alternative remedy).

[In n.46 delete "; R (on the application of C) v Financial Services Authority [2012] EWHC (Admin) at [83], [90]–[93] (Upper Tribunal had no power to order the Defendant to comply with its statutory duty to give reasons)"]

[Add to end of n.46]

See also *R. (on the application of Willford) v Financial Services Authority* [2013] EWCA Civ 677 at [36].

Alternative Dispute Resolution (ADR)

[In n.79 delete "(May 2012)" and substitute] 16–022

(August 2014)

[In n.82 delete "(May 2012)" and substitute]

(August 2014)

[Add to end of n.82]

In *PGF II SA v OMFS Co 1 Ltd* [2013] EWCA Civ 1288; [2014] 1 W.L.R. 1386 at [34]–[40], the CA extended the guidance given by the CA in *Halsey v Milton Keynes General NHS Trust* [2004] EWCA Civ 576; [2004] 1 W.L.R. 3002 to the effect that, in general, a party's silence in the face of an invitation to participate in ADR was itself unreasonable regardless of whether or not refusal to engage in ADR might have been reasonable.

Gathering evidence and information

The duty of candour

[In n.95 delete "http://www.tsol.gov.uk" and substitute] 16–027

https://www.gov.uk/government/organisations/treasury-solicitor-s-department

Freedom of Information Act 2000

[In n.99 delete "3rd edn (2010)" and substitute] 16–028

4th edn (2014)

[Add to start of list of cases in n.105] 16–030

Kennedy v Information Commissioner [2014] UKSC 20; [2014] 2 W.L.R. 808 (on documents created by or provided to a public body relating to an inquiry conducted by that body);

[Add to end of n.105]

The CA overturned the exercise of the Attorney General's veto in relation to correspondence between the Prince of Wales and government departments on the ground that mere disagreement with the conclusions of the Upper Tribunal was not a sufficient basis for the exercise of the veto (*R. (on the application of Evans) v Attorney General* [2014] EWCA Civ 254; [2014] 2 W.L.R. 1334 at [36]–[39]). On the use of a closed material procedure under the 2000 Act, see *Browning v Information Commissioner* [2014] EWCA Civ 1050 at [31]–[36].

Environmental Information Regulations 2004

16–031 *[Add to end of n.106]*

The power to veto a decision to disclose information under the 2000 Act must be exercised compatibly with EU law (*R. (on the application of Evans) v Attorney General* [2014] EWCA Civ 254; [2014] 2 W.L.R. 1334 at [52]–[67]).

Preparing the Claim Form

16–036 *[In n.116 delete the final sentence and substitute]*

The fee is £140: Civil Proceedings Fees (Amendment) Order (2014/874), Sch.1.

16–037 *[Add to end of n.121]*

In *R. (on the application of Gul) v Secretary of State for Justice* [2014] EWHC 373 (Admin) at [41]–[44], the DC made two important observations on the obligations of claimants: to give full and frank disclosure of matters which may undermine their case (failure to do so may lead to relief being refused); and to reconsider the merits of the claim on receipt of the defendant's evidence (which may have costs consequences).

Permission

The purpose of the permission stage

16–048 *[Add to n.147 after ". . . of applications overall"]*

This figure rose to 92 per cent in 2013 (Ministry of Justice, *Court Statistics Quarterly January to March 2014* (June 19, 2014).

Criteria on which permission is granted or refused

[Add new para.16–049A after 16–049]   **16–049**

The Criminal Justice and Courts Bill 2014 (if passed in its present form) will   **16–049A**
introduce a new criterion at the permission stage. If the court considers it
"highly likely" that "the outcome for the applicant" would not "have been
substantially different if the conduct complained of had not occurred" then it
must refuse permission.[154a] The court may consider this question of its own
motion, but it must do so if the defendant requests that it does.[154b] The senior
judiciary's response to the Government's consultation warns of "Dress rehearsal
permission hearings" involving "detailed consideration of the facts".[154c]

[154a] Criminal Justice and Courts Bill 2014 s.70(2), inserting new subss 3B
and 3C into Senior Courts Act 1981 s.31. See para.18–049A.

[154b] Section 70(2).

[154c] "Response of the Senior Judiciary to the Ministry of Justice's
Consultation entitled 'Judicial Review: Proposals for Further Reform'"
(November 1, 2013) at 22.

The timing of the application for permission

[Add to end of n.172]   **16–054**

The views of the Compliance Committee have no direct legal consequences
in domestic law (*R. (on the application of Evans) v Secretary of State for
Communities and Local Government* [2013] EWCA Civ 114; [2013] J.P.L.
1027 at [37]–[38]).

[Add to end of n.174]   **16–055**

In *R. (on the application of Nash) v Barnet LBC* [2013] EWCA Civ 1004;
[2013] P.T.S.R. 1457 at [54]–[65], the CA distinguished *Burkett* and held
that the crucial question was not when the decision was finally or irrevocably
made, but when the relevant duty (in this case to consult) properly arose.
The decisions in the present case were not provisional and each stage might
have significant consequences.

[Add to end of n.178]   **16–056**

See paras 16–061A and 17–028 on the new Planning Court.

[Add new para.16–061A after para.16–061]   **16–061**

In claims for judicial review where the grounds arose after July 1, 2013: (1)   **16–061A**
a claim for judicial review of a planning decision by the Secretary of State or

the local planning authority under the planning Acts as defined must be brought within six weeks of the date when the application first arose; and (2) a claim for judicial review of a decision to award a contract to which the Public Contracts Regulations 2006 (SI 2006/5) apply must be brought within 30 days beginning with the date when the claimant first knew or ought to have known that grounds for challenging the decision had arisen.[198a]

[198a] CPR r.54.5 (as amended by Civil Procedure (Amendment No. 4) Rules 2013/1412, r.4).

Challenging the refusal of permission

16–063 *[Add to para.16–063 after ". . . at a hearing.[202]"]*

Where a claim is filed on or after July 2013 and the court refuses permission to proceed and records the fact that the application is totally without merit in accordance with CPR r.23.12, the claimant cannot request that the decision be reconsidered at an oral hearing.

[In n.202 delete "CPR r.54.12(3)–(5)" and substitute]

CPR r.54.12(3)–(5) and (7). The fee for a request for reconsideration is £350.

[In n.202 delete final sentence]

16–065 *[In n.207 delete "PD 52, para.4.13" and substitute]*

PD 52C, para.15(2)

Interlocutory Stage

16–067 *[Delete all text in n.213 and substitute]*

£700 (from April 2014), Civil Proceedings Fees (Amendment) Order 2014, Sch.1. If the claimant has already paid the fee of £350 for an oral hearing, the fee is a further £350.

Applications by interveners

16–068 *[Add to end of n.216]*

The Government is proposing that interveners should be prevented from seeking their costs from the parties and should bear any costs caused by their intervention (see n.279).

Disclosure

[Add to end of para.16–069]   16–069

The court may order pre-action disclosure in judicial review proceedings pursuant to CPR r.31.16(3), although such applications will "rarely" be successful.[218a]

[218a] See *British Union for the Abolition of Vivisection (BUAV) v Secretary of State for the Home Department* [2014] EWHC 43 (Admin); [2014] A.C.D. 69 at [32]–[34], [54]–[67].

[In n.220 delete final sentence and substitute]   16–070

Section 17 of the Justice and Security Act 2013 provides that the court may not exercise its *Norwich Pharmacal* jurisdiction in relation to "sensitive information", which is information: (a) held by an intelligence service; (b) obtained from, or held on behalf of, an intelligence service; (c) derived in whole or part from information obtained from, or held on behalf of, an intelligence service; (d) relating to an intelligence service; or (e) specified or described in a certificate issued by the Secretary of State in relation to the proceedings as information which the disclosing party should not be ordered to disclose. The Secretary of State may issue such a certificate if she considers that it would be contrary to the public interest to disclose: (i) the information; (ii) whether the information exists; or (iii) whether the disclosing party has the information. A disclosure is contrary to the public interest if it would cause damage to the interests of national security or to the interests of the international relations of the United Kingdom.

Preparation of skeleton arguments

[Add to end of n.234]   16–073

See also *Standard Bank v Via Mat International* [2013] EWCA Civ 490; [2013] 2 All E.R. (Comm) 1222 at [26]–[27].

The full hearing

[Add to end of n.244]   16–078

Ermakov was followed and treated as an important statement of principle by the CA in *R. (on the application of Lanner Parish Council) v Cornwall Council* [2013] EWCA Civ 1290 at [59]–[66].

Appeals after the full hearing

Appeals in civil judicial review claims

16–082   *[Add to end of n.253]*

The Government proposes that the circumstances in which an appeal may "leapfrog" to the SC should be expanded by removing the requirement that all parties should consent to it and setting out alternative conditions which are that there is a point of law of general public importance and: either the proceedings relate to a matter of national importance; or the proceedings are so significant that the judge considers a hearing by the SC is justified; or the judge considers that the benefit of the matter being considered by the SC outweighs those of it being heard by the CA (see Pt 3 of the Criminal Justice and Courts Bill). The Bill would also permit appeals to "leapfrog" to the SC from the Upper Tribunal in similar circumstances.

Funding judicial review

16–083   *[Delete all text in n.256 and substitute]*

As of August 4, 2014, the application fee for permission to apply for judicial review is £140. There is a fee of £350 for a request for oral renewal of an application for permission. For judicial review after permission is granted, the fee is £700, or £350 if permission was granted after oral renewal of the application (Civil Proceedings Fees Order 2008/1053 (as amended)).

[In n.257 delete "Multiplying these figures by 1.3 would provide the 2013 values" and substitute]

Multiplying these figures by 1.34 would provide the 2014 values.

16–084   *[Delete all text in para.16–084, but retain all footnotes, and substitute]*

For most claimants, this expense is prohibitive and judicial review litigation cannot be pursued without some form of public funding. The provision of public funding for judicial review has undergone profound change. The old system was based on the Community Legal Service (CLS) Fund administered by the Legal Services Commission (LSC).[258] Since April 1, 2013, the new system has operated under the Legal Aid, Sentencing and Punishment of Offenders Act 2012.[259]

The functions previously discharged by the LSC are now within the remit of the Lord Chancellor, and individual decisions to award legal aid are taken by the Director of Legal Aid Casework as part of the Legal Aid Agency (an executive agency of the Ministry of Justice).[260] Civil legal aid is available for legal services which fall within Pt 1 of Sch.1 to the 2012 Act and where the Director has determined that the individual qualifies for the relevant services.

Schedule 1 includes "judicial review of an enactment, decision, act or omission", habeas corpus, deliberate or dishonest abuse by a public authority of its position or powers which results in reasonably foreseeable harm to a person or property and a significant breach of Convention rights.[261] However, this is subject to the specific exclusion of services provided to an individual which do not have the potential to produce a benefit for the individual, a member of his family or the environment.[262] The requirement of benefit has the obvious potential to reduce the availability of legal aid for public interest challenges. It is also questionable whether a claimant whose only remedy would be a declaration of incompatibility under the HRA is likely to qualify. If a claimant falls outside of these provisions, he must rely on the Director's discretion to make an exceptional case determination where the legal services are necessary to avoid a breach of the individual's Convention rights or enforceable EU law rights.[263]

The Director's determination that an individual qualifies for the legal services described above is governed by: the financial resources of the individual and the criteria to be established by the Lord Chancellor to reflect the likely cost of providing the services; the importance of the matter to the individual; the seriousness of the act or omission subject to challenge; the prospects of success; other means of resolving the dispute; and the public interest.[264] Regulations now provide for appeals to an adjudicator against the Director's Determinations.[265]

[Add to end of n.263]

In *Gudanaviciene v Director of Legal Aid* [2014] EWHC 1840 (Admin), the court overturned a number of decisions of the Director in cases involving art.8 of the ECHR on the basis that they were too restrictive.

[Delete all text in n.264 and substitute]

Legal Aid, Sentencing and Punishment of Offenders Act 2012 s.11. The Civil Legal Aid (Merits Criteria) Regulations 2013 (2013/104) reg.75 requires that an individual has exhausted all reasonable alternatives to bringing proceedings, including any complaints system, ombudsman scheme or other form of alternative dispute resolution. This goes further than the previous law, which only required alternatives to be exhausted if they provided an effective remedy. See further, the Civil Legal Aid (Merits Criteria) (Amendment) Regulations 2014 (2014/131). The Government's response to its 2013 Consultation contains further proposals for savings of £218 million per annum by 2018/2019 (*Transforming Legal Aid – Next Steps: Government Response* (February 27, 2014)). The Government also proposes that legal aid will only be paid in cases where permission is ultimately granted, subject to the discretion of the Legal Aid Agency. The attempt to introduce a residence test for legal aid by delegated legislation was found to be unlawful in *R. (on the application of the Public Law Project) v Secretary of State for Justice* [2014] EWHC 2365 (Admin).

[Delete all text in n.265 and substitute]

Civil Legal Aid (Procedure) Regulations (2012/3098) regs 28, 45–48, 53, 59.

Costs

16–086 *[Add to n.267 before "The Civil Procedure Rules . . ."]*

The SC considered the CJEU's response and decided that the following factors were relevant to the ultimate level of recovery by the defendant: (i) whether the claim had a reasonable prospect of success; (ii) the importance of what is at stake for the claimant; (iii) the importance of what is at stake for the protection of the environment; (iv) the complexity of the relevant law and procedure (in that greater complexity is likely to require higher expenditure by the defendants); and the potentially frivolous nature of the claim at its various stages: *R. (on the application of Edwards) v Environment Agency (No.2)* [2013] UKSC 78; [2014] 1 W.L.R. 55 at [28].

[In n.273 delete "CPR r.44.3(5)" and substitute]

CPR r.44.4

[Delete final sentence of para.16–086 and substitute]

Since April 2013, the success fee under such an agreement is no longer recoverable from the losing party.

[Add to end of n.279]

The Government proposes that a party to judicial review proceedings may not be required to pay an intervener's costs and the court must order an intervener to pay a party's costs if they have been incurred as a result of the intervener's involvement in the proceedings (in both cases unless there are exceptional circumstances that make it inappropriate to do so) (Criminal Justice and Courts Bill cl.73).

Protective costs orders in public interest cases

16–089 *[Add to end of n.289]*

See further *R. (on the application of Litvinenko) v Secretary of State for the Home Department* [2013] EWHC 3135 (Admin); [2014] A.C.D. 25 at [18]–[26]. Note that the Divisional Court in *Litvinenko* appeared to consider that the *Corner House* principles only apply to "exceptional cases" (at [32]). As the Administrative Court observed in *R. (on the application of the Plantagenet Alliance) v Secretary of State for Justice* [2013] EWHC 3164 (Admin); [2014] A.C.D. 26 at [28], any "exceptionality" requirement would be contrary to the approach in the CA in *Buglife* and *Morgan*.

[Add to end of n.296]   16–090

The Government proposes to place PCOs on an exclusive statutory footing in the Criminal Justice and Courts Bill. They will be called "costs capping orders" and will only be available if permission to apply for judicial review has been granted. This is a major change which is likely drastically to limit the usefulness of such orders since defendants often incur very substantial costs before permission is granted and claimants would be exposed to these costs in full. The list of factors relevant to the grant of a costs capping order which are set out in the Bill substantially reflect the current law, but the Bill grants the Lord Chancellor the power to amend the list of relevant factors by means of regulations.

Costs before and at the permission stage

[Add to end of n.303]   16–092

In *R. (on the application of Smoke Club Ltd) v Network Rail Infrastructure Ltd* [2013] EWHC 3830 (Admin); [2014] 2 Costs L.O. 123, the Administrative Court declined to follow the usual rules on costs after discontinuance in CPR r.38.6(1) on the basis that special considerations apply to judicial review cases. The court awarded the defendant a proportion of their costs after the Acknowledgement of Service to reflect the fact that the claimant had renewed a hopeless claim and produced fresh evidence which put the defendant to additional expense before the claim was withdrawn.

[Add to end of n.304]

The Government proposes to invite the Civil Procedure Rule Committee to introduce a principle that the defendant's costs of attending an oral permission hearing should usually be recoverable from the claimant (see para.1–005A).

Costs when a claim is discontinued after permission

[Add to end of n.311]   16–095

There is new Guidance for judicial review cases in which the parties have agreed to settle the claim but are unable to agree liability for costs and have submitted that issue for determination by the court: *http://www. justice.gov.uk/downloads/courts/administrative-court/aco-costs-guidance-dec-13.pdf.*

CHAPTER 17

OTHER JUDICIAL REVIEW PROCEEDINGS

JUDICIAL REVIEW AND TRIBUNALS

[In n.14 delete "In 2011 . . . Table 7.12)" and substitute] 17–004

In 2012, 85 per cent of applications for permission to apply for judicial review concerned immigration or asylum matters: over 10,000 applications were received, 31 per cent of which were found to be totally without merit (Ministry of Justice, *Court Statistics Quarterly July to September 2013*, pp.29–34).

[Add to end of n.17] 17–005

The Upper Tribunal cannot review its own decision to refuse permission to appeal and the only remedy in such cases is for the party aggrieved to seek judicial review of the Upper Tribunal's refusal (*Samuda v Secretary of State for Work and Pensions* [2014] EWCA Civ 1; [2014] 3 All E.R. 201 at [13]).

Judicial review in the Upper Tribunal

[Add to end of n.18] 17–006

On appeal from decisions of the Upper Tribunal in cases involving judicial review of First-tier Tribunal decisions, the appellate court should exercise restraint and permit flexibility to the Upper Tribunal to develop guidance on the specialised area of law concerned in order to promote consistency (*R. (on the application of Jones) v First-tier Tribunal* [2013] UKSC 19; [2013] 2 A.C. 48 at [26], [42]–[43]).

[Add to end of n.19]

The Upper Tribunal has produced its own Judicial Review standard forms for statements of case (and guidance on them), which are available at *http://www.justice.gov.uk/tribunals/immigration-asylum-upper/application-for-judicial-review*. The Upper Tribunal has also produced guideline judgments on, for example, how it will deal with immigration judicial reviews where the Secretary of State has failed to submit an Acknowledgement of Service within the time limit required by the Tribunal Procedure (Upper Tribunal)

Rules 2008 (*R. (on the application of Kumar) v Secretary of State for the Home Department* [2014] UKUT 00104). See the additional guideline judgments on the claimant's continuing duty to re-assess the claim in light of developments (*R. (on the application of Mahmood) v Secretary of State for the Home Department* [2014] UKUT 00439 (IAC)).

[Delete all text in n.20 and substitute]

In outline, they are: the application does not seek relief beyond the ordinary judicial review remedies; does not question anything done by the Crown Court; and falls within a class specified by the Lord Chief Justice. Section 31A of the Senior Courts Act 1981 provides for mandatory transfer if all three conditions are met. The Lord Chief Justice has so far identified the following such classes of case: decisions of the First-tier Tribunal on an appeal under the Criminal Injuries Compensation Scheme; where the First-tier Tribunal has declined to review one of its decisions and there is no right of appeal (Practice Direction (Upper Tribunal: Judicial Review Jurisdiction) [2009] 1 W.L.R. 327); and, as of 1 November 2013, any decision made under the Immigration Acts or otherwise relating to leave to enter or remain in the UK outside the immigration rules and a decision of the Immigration and Asylum Chamber of the First-tier Tribunal from which no appeal lies to the Upper Tribunal (except where the application includes: a challenge to the validity of primary or subordinate legislation; a challenge to the lawfulness of detention; a challenge to a decision on citizenship; a challenge to a decision of the Upper Tribunal; an application for a declaration of incompatibility under the HRA (and certain other matters specified in the Direction)) (Direction given in accordance with Pt 1 of Sch.2 to the Constitutional Reform Act 2005 and s.18 of the Tribunals, Courts and Enforcement Act 2007, August 21, 2013). In *Ashraf v Secretary of State for the Home Department* [2013] EWHC 4028 (Admin) at [2], the court indicated that it may well be treated as an abuse of process to issue judicial review proceedings challenging removal in the Administrative Court on the basis of an unmeritorious claim of unlawful detention.

HABEAS CORPUS

17–007 *[Add to end of n.24]*

There was a violation of art.5(4) in a case where the detained individual lacked capacity to instruct a lawyer to seek a remedy and where her nearest relative was barred from doing so (*MH v UK* (2014) 58 E.H.R.R. 35).

17–009 *[Add to end of n.37]*

This outcome is unaffected by the decision of the ECtHR in *James, Lee and Wells v UK* (2013) 56 E.H.R.R. 12.

Applications to Quash Certain Orders, etc.

Procedure

[Add new para.17–028A after para.17–028] **17–028**

The Administrative Court now has a new specialist list called the Planning **17–028A**
Court governed by CPR Pt 54.21–24 and Practice Direction 54E.[96a] The
Planning Court will hear all claims lodged after April 6, 2014 (or transferred
to it after that date) which involve a judicial review or statutory challenge to
planning and some environmental decisions.[96b] Significant Planning Court
claims will be dealt with according to the target time scales set out in the
Practice Direction.[96c]

[96a] The proposal to establish the Planning Court appeared in Ch.3 of Ministry
of Justice, *Judicial Review: Proposals for Further Reform*, Cm 8703 (September
2013). The Government's aim was stated to be to streamline the legal process
for determining challenges in order to reduce the extent to which such challenges unduly hinder economic development and regeneration.

[96b] A Planning Court claim includes a judicial review or statutory challenge to:
planning permission or other development consents; the enforcement of planning control and the enforcement of other statutory schemes; applications
under the Transport and Works Act 1992; wayleaves; highways and other rights
of way; compulsory purchase orders; village greens; European Union environmental legislation and domestic transpositions, including assessments for development consents, habitats, waste and pollution control; national, regional or
other planning policy documents; and any other matter which the Planning
Liaison Judge considers appropriate. The Planning Liaison Judge will be nominated by the President of the Queen's Bench Division who will also nominate
specialist planning judges to deal with significant Planning Court claims.

[96c] Significant Planning Court claims are defined in Practice Direction
54EPD3.2 as those: relating to developments with significant economic
impact either locally or more broadly; which raise important points of law;
which generate significant public interest; or by virtue of the volume or
nature of the technical material are best dealt with by judges with significant
experience of handling such matters. It is for the Planning Liaison Judge to
designate claims as significant.

Coroners

[Delete "inquisition" in n.116 and substitute] **17–034**

Record of Inquest

17–035 *[In para.17–035 delete "inquisition" and substitute]*

Record of Inquest

[Add to end of n.119]

Judicial review will remain available for those decisions which cannot be challenged under s.13 of the 1998 Act such as those made in advance of the hearing and those relating to the actual conduct of the proceedings.

[Add to end of n.120]

On the relevant costs principles, see *R. (on the application of Davis) v Birmingham Deputy Coroner* [2004] 1 W.L.R. 2739 at [47] and *R. (on the application of Medihani) v HM Coroner for Inner South District of Greater London* [2012] EWHC 1104 (Admin); [2012] A.C.D. 63 at [59]–[64].

17–036 *[Delete all text in para.17–036, but retain all footnotes, and substitute]*

With effect from July 25, 2013 (and subject to the exception described below), the Coroners Act 1988 has been repealed by the Coroners and Justices Act 2009. Under the 2009 Act, a new post of Chief Coroner of England and Wales has been created.[121] The main responsibilities of the Chief Coroner include: to set national standards for all coroners (including new inquest rules); to oversee the implementation of the 2009 Act; to maintain a register of coroner investigations which last more than 12 months; and to take steps to reduce unnecessary delays and monitor investigations into the death of service personnel. As originally enacted in the 2009 Act, s.13 of the 1988 Act was to be replaced by a statutory right of appeal to the new post of Chief Coroner. However, the provisions of the 2009 Act creating the new right of appeal have now themselves been repealed on grounds of cost and s.13 of the 1988 Act and judicial review remain the mechanisms for challenge.

EVALUATION OF JUDICIAL REVIEW PROCEDURES

The role of the court in judicial review

Questions of law

17–040 *[Add to end of n.134]*

The courts have adopted a functional, rather than principled, approach to defining what constitutes a question of law for the purposes of the powers of the Upper Tribunal; with the aims of allowing the Upper Tribunal scope to provide guidance in the interests of consistency while retaining a sufficient level of scrutiny by the ordinary courts to protect the rule of law (*R. (on the application of Cart) v Upper Tribunal* [2011] UKSC 28; [2012] 1 A.C. 663 and *R. (on the application of Jones) v First-tier Tribunal* [2013] UKSC 19; [2013] 2 A.C. 48 at [41]–[46] in which Lord Carnwath describes the distinction between law and fact as a matter of policy or expediency). See D. Feldman, "Error of Law and Flawed Administrative Acts" [2014] C.L.J. 275.

The different interests of those affected by judicial review

[Add to end of n.147]   17–049

See para.1–005 and Ch.16 for the latest Government proposals.

Chapter 18

JUDICIAL REVIEW REMEDIES

Interim Remedies

Bail

[Add to end of n.63] 18–022

The court may also permit judicial review where the decision-maker took into account a legally irrelevant factor: *R. (on the application of U) v Northampton Crown Court* [2013] EWHC 4519 (Admin) at [12]. A defendant on trial on indictment in the Crown Court may not challenge a decision to revoke bail made in the midst of a trial: *R. (on the application of Uddin) v Crown Court at Leeds* [2013] EWHC 2752 (Admin); [2014] 1 W.L.R. 1742 at [35].

Final Remedial Orders

[Add to end of n.71] 18–023

If the Criminal Justice and Courts Bill 2014 is passed in its present form, the Administrative Court will be required to refuse to grant relief where "it appears to the court to be highly likely that the outcome for the applicant would not have been substantially different if the conduct complained of had not occurred". This would involve a lower threshold than the current law which requires that the same result would almost inevitably have been reached and removes the court's discretion (see para.18–049A).

Discretion in Granting and Withholding Remedies

Presumption in favour of relief

[Add new title and new para.18–049A after 18–049] 18–049

Substantially different outcome

18–049A The Criminal Justice and Courts Bill 2014 (which is before Parliament at the time of writing) will define the circumstances in which the High Court *must* refuse relief. Clause 70 of the Bill provides that the High Court must refuse to grant relief on an application for judicial review, and may not make any award under the Senior Courts Act 1981 s.31(4), if "it appears to the court to be highly likely that the outcome for the applicant would not have been substantially different if the conduct complained of had not occurred".[127a] The concept of "highly likely" is novel, and marks a significant departure from the test of inevitability currently applied at common law as a basis for refusing a remedy.[127b] It appears that the judge will be required to consider the significance of the alleged legal defect to the decision in question and speculate as to what the outcome would have been if the defect had not occurred. The courts have historically sought to avoid engaging in such questions.[127c] The constitutional implications of this aspect of the Bill have been strongly criticised.[127d]

[127a] Criminal Justice and Courts Bill 2014 cl.70, inserting a new subs.2A into s.31 of the Senior Courts Act 1981.

[127b] See para.18–056.

[127c] See n.148

[127d] See, e.g. B. Jaffey and T. Hickman, "Loading the Dice in Judicial Review: The Criminal Justice and Courts Bill 2014", UK Const L. Blog (February 6, 2014), *http://ukconstitutionallaw.org/2014/02/06/ben-jaffey-and-tom-hickman-loading-the-dice-in-judicial-review-the-criminal-justice-and-courts-bill-2014/*.

Claimant has suffered no harm

18–056 *[Delete all text in para.18–056 and substitute]*

In some cases, the court has withheld a remedy from a claimant on the basis that he has been caused no harm (the term "prejudice" is often used) by the unlawful act of the public authority.[146] Under this head, a minor technical breach of a statutory requirement may be too insignificant to justify relief. The court has also taken into account the fact that the public authority would have made the same decision even if the legal flaw had not occurred.[147] The Criminal Justice and Courts Bill 2014 will replace this discretion with a requirement to refuse relief if "it appears to the court to be highly likely that the outcome for the applicant would not have been substantially different if

the conduct complained of had not occurred".[147a] In the past, the Law
Commission, academic commentators and the court have all warned of the
difficulties and risks in prejudging decisions, including overstepping the
bounds of the court's reviewing functions.[148]

[147a] Clause 70. See para.18–049A.

Nullity and ultra vires and discretion

[Add to end of n.151]   18–058

See further, D. Feldman: "Error of Law and Flawed Administrative Acts"
[2014] C.L.J. 275.

CHAPTER 19

MONETARY REMEDIES IN JUDICIAL REVIEW

PROCEDURAL ISSUES

Civil claim or judicial review?

Public law issues must be decided to determine damages claim

[Add to end of n.22]   19–009

This paragraph and para.19–025 were found to be "fully justified by authority" in *Tchenguiz v Director of the Serious Fraud Office* [2014] EWCA Civ 472 at [14]. The case concerned the question whether a concession that search orders had been unlawful in public law proceedings prevented the defendant from relying on defences to a private law claim. The CA found that the defendant was entitled to resist the private law claim.

DEFENDANTS IN MONETARY CLAIMS RELATING TO JUDICIAL REVIEW

[Add to n.29 before "In Adams v Law Society . . ."]   19–012

This decision was applied to render the Ministry of Justice vicariously liable for injury caused to an employee by a prisoner working in a prison kitchen in *Cox v Ministry of Justice* [2014] EWCA Civ 132; [2014] I.C.R. 713 at [42]–[48]. In contrast, the Chief Constable was not vicariously liable for acts of personal harassment carried out by one of his officers in relation to the officer's former partner in *Allen v Chief Constable of Hampshire* [2013] EWCA Civ 967 at [28]–[35].

[In n.35 delete "NHS act 1977 s.125" and substitute]   19–013

NHS Act 2006 s.69

The Crown as a defendant

[In n.53 delete "[2011] EWHC 1676 (QB) at [95]–[109]" and substitute]   19–016

[2013] UKSC 41; [2014] A.C. 52 at [89]–[96]

[In n.53 delete "R. (on the application of Smith . . . at [19]–[20]" and substitute]

Al-Skeini v UK (2011) 53 E.H.R.R. 18

Judicial Immunity from civil liability

19–018   *[Add to end of n.60]*

See further, J. Murphy, "Rethinking Tortious Immunity for Judicial Acts" (2013) 33 L.S. 455 (arguing that the same test for liability should apply to superior court judges as in the tort of misfeasance in public office).

[Add to n.63 after ". . . power to make binding decisions"]

In *Singh v Reading BC* [2013] EWCA Civ 909; [2013] 1 W.L.R. 3052 at [43]–[46] and [70]–[72], the CA declined to follow *Heath* and held that the immunity did not apply to a claim for constructive dismissal by a former employee where the allegation was that the employer had placed undue pressure on another employee to produce an untrue witness statement.

[In n.64 delete "P. Milmo . . . (2008)" and substitute]

R. Parkes and A. Mullis et al, *Gatley on Libel and Slander*, 12th edn (2013)

Tribunals

19–023   *[Add to end of n.85]*

Heath was not followed in *Singh v Reading BC* [2013] EWCA Civ 909; [2013] 1 W.L.R. 3052 at [43]–[46].

The reason for immunity

19–024   *[Delete "the immunity of the Crown" and substitute]*

Judicial immunity

[In n.88 delete "10th edn (2009), p.703" and substitute]

11th edn (2014), p.697

[Add to end of n.123]

See further, *Furnell v Flaherty* [2013] EWHC 377 (QB).

[In n.124 delete "4th edn (2006), pp.72–77" and substitute]

8th edn (2013), pp.70–83

Negligence

[Add to end of n.140]   19–038

Applying *Caparo*, it was not fair, just and reasonable to impose a duty of care on officers engaged in apprehending a suspected drug dealer on the street in relation to a bystander who suffered physical injury as a result of negligence by the officers (*Robinson v Chief Constable of West Yorkshire* [2014] EWCA Civ 15 at [44]–[51]). The SC decided that the question of whether it was fair, just and reasonable to impose a duty of care in relation to the deaths of British troops in Iraq arising from a failure to provide suitable equipment should be determined on the evidence at trial, but indicated that the defence of combat immunity should be narrowly construed (*Smith v Ministry of Defence* [2012] UKSC 41; [2014] A.C. 52 at [89]–[101]). The SC held it was fair, just and reasonable to impose a non-delegable duty of care on a school in relation to severe brain damage suffered by a pupil during a school swimming lesson (*Woodland v Swimming Teachers Association* [2013] UKSC 66; [2014] A.C. 537 at [25]).

[Add to end of n.148]   19–041

See further, D. Nolan, "Varying the Standard of Care in Negligence" [2013] C.L.J. 651.

[In n.154 delete "strongly doubted in . . . 863 at [47]" and substitute]   19–043

distinguished in *MacDonald v Aberdeenshire Council* [2013] CSIH 83 at [42]

[Add to end of n.172]   19–045

See further, J. Hartshorne, "Contemporary Approaches Towards Pure Economic Loss in the Law of Negligence" [2014] J.B.L. 425.

MISFEASANCE IN PUBLIC OFFICE

[Add to end of n.186]

In *Crawford Adjusters (Cayman) Ltd v Sagicor General Insurance (Cayman) Ltd* [2013] UKPC 17; [2014] A.C. 366, the PC held that there continued to be a tort of the malicious prosecution of civil proceedings where malice and the absence of reasonable cause could be shown. The tort does not apply to disciplinary proceedings: *Gregory v Portsmouth City Council* [2000] 1 A.C. 419.

DEPRIVATION OF LIBERTY: FALSE IMPRIONMENT

19–056 *[Add to end of n.235]*

The detention of a prisoner beyond the period when he would have been released had his case been considered speedily in accordance with art.5(4) of the ECHR does not constitute false imprisonment as his detention continues to be lawful as a matter of domestic law (*R. (on the application of Sturnham) v Parole Board* [2013] UKSC 23; [2013] 2 A.C. 254 at [15]–[16]).

MEASURE OF DAMAGES IN TORT

19–061 *[In n.248 delete "18th edn (2011)" and substitute]*

19th edn (2014)

COMPENSATION UNDER THE HUMAN RIGHTS ACT

Principles

19–084 *[Delete "R. (on the application of Faulkner . . . [103]" and substitute]*

R. (on the application of Sturnham) v Parole Board [2013] UKSC 23; [2013] 2 A.C. 254 at [99]–[103]. The court should be provided with an agreed schedule of the relevant authorities: stating the violations of the ECHR which were established and the sum awarded; summarising the parties submissions on them; listing the authorities in chronological order; and explaining the principles which are said to derive from them.

[Add to end of n.309]

In *Sturnham* [2013] UKSC 23; [2013] 2 A.C. 254 at [29], the SC indicated that reference to the ECtHR case law is likely to diminish as the award of damages under s.8 of the HRA becomes "naturalised".

[Add to end of n.314]

The ECtHR set out some guidance on its approach to awarding just satisfaction in *Agrokompleks v Ukraine* (App. No.23465/03) (July 25, 2013) at [76]–[81]. In *Al-Jedda v UK* (2011) 53 E.H.R.R. 789 at [114], the ECtHR stated that its function was not "akin to a domestic tort mechanism court in apportioning fault and compensatory damages . . . [i]ts guiding principle is equity, which above all involves flexibility". The focus of the domestic court should be on the practice of the ECtHR, which tends not to provide "articulated statements of principle" in relation to awards (*R. (on the application of Sturnham) v Parole Board* [2013] UKSC 23; [2013] 2 A.C. 254 at [13], [31]–[32]). The domestic court should focus on ECtHR cases involving applicants from the UK or countries with a comparable cost of living (*Sturnham* [2013] UKSC 23; [2013] 2 A.C. 254 at [38]–[39]). It is questionable whether this should apply to the non-pecuniary elements of loss.

[Add to end of point (d) in para.19–084]

The ECtHR's case law on awards for loss of opportunity is inconsistent.[317a]

[317a] *McGregor on Damages*, 19th edn (2014) paras 48–057 to 48–064. In *Sturnham* [2013] UKSC 23; [2013] 2 A.C. 254 at [13], the SC held that damages should be awarded where it is established on the balance of probabilities that a violation of art.5(4) has resulted in the detention of a prisoner beyond the date when he would otherwise have been released.

[Add to end of n.319]

Sturnham [2013] UKSC 23; [2013] 2 A.C. 254 at [41], [53]–[54]. *McGregor on Damages*, 19th edn (2014) para.48–055 has a useful table of ECtHR awards for non-pecuniary losses.

[Add to end of n.320]

Claims for damages under arts 3 and 8 of the ECHR brought under s.7 of the HRA relating to the conduct of undercover police officers in entering into intimate physical relationships with the claimants had to be brought before the Investigatory Powers Tribunal established by the Regulation of Investigatory Powers Act 2000 and not in the High Court (*AKJ v Commissioner of Police of the Metropolis* [2013] EWCA Civ 1342; [2014] 1 W.L.R. 285 at [37]–[43]). The common law claims for deceit, assault, misfeasance in public office and negligence were permitted to proceed before the High Court and the stay granted below was lifted (at [65]).

Individual Convention rights

Article 5 (right to liberty and security)

19–091 *[Delete all text in para.19–091 and substitute]*

In *R. (on the application of Sturnham) v Parole Board*,[334] the Supreme Court held that where it was demonstrated on a balance of probabilities that a violation of art.5(4) has resulted in the detention of a prisoner beyond the date when he would otherwise have been released, damages should be awarded with pecuniary losses being compensated in full. Non-pecuniary losses for frustration and anxiety should be awarded if sufficiently severe and this will usually be the case where the delay was of three months or more.

[334] [2013] UKSC 23; [2013] 2 A.C. 254 at [67]–[76].

19–093 *[Add to end of para.19–093]*

The Supreme Court reduced this sum on appeal to £6,500.

[In n.336 delete "(appeal pending)" and substitute]

(CA) and [2013] UKSC 23; [2013] 2 A.C. 254 at [87] (SC).

19–100 *[Add new heading and new para.19–100A after para.19–100]*

First Protocol, art.3 (right to free elections)

19–100A In *Firth v United Kingdom*,[358a] the ECtHR confirmed that a declaration that the automatic ban on voting by prisoners violated the right to free elections constituted just satisfaction and declined to award any compensation.

[358a] (App. No.47794/09) (August 12, 2014).

Appendices

Appendices

APPENDIX C

[Insert new version of s.31A of the Senior Courts Act 1981]

31A Transfer of judicial review applications to Upper Tribunal

(1)   This section applies where an application is made to the High Court–

    (a)   for judicial review, or

    (b)   for permission to apply for judicial review.

(2)   If Conditions 1, 2 and 3[1] are met, the High Court must by order transfer the application to the Upper Tribunal.

(3)   If Conditions 1 and 2[2] are met, but Condition 3 is not, the High Court may by order transfer the application to the Upper Tribunal if it appears to the High Court to be just and convenient to do so.

(4)   Condition 1 is that the application does not seek anything other than–

    (a)   relief under section 31(1)(a) and (b);

    (b)   permission to apply for relief under section 31(1)(a) and (b);

    (c)   an award under section 31(4);

    (d)   interest;

    (e)   costs.

(5)   Condition 2 is that the application does not call into question anything done by the Crown Court.

(6)   Condition 3 is that the application falls within a class specified under section 18(6) of the Tribunals, Courts and Enforcement Act 2007.

---

[1] Words substituted by Crime and Courts Act 2013 c. 22 Pt 2 s.22(1)(a) (November 1, 2013).

[2] Words substituted by Crime and Courts Act 2013 c. 22 Pt 2 s.22(1)(c) (November 1, 2013).

APPENDIX F

[Insert new version of CPR 54]

PART 54 – JUDICIAL REVIEW AND STATUTORY REVIEW

I JUDICIAL REVIEW

Scope and interpretation

54.1 (1) This Section of this Part contains rules about judicial review.

(2) In this Section –

    (a) a 'claim for judicial review' means a claim to review the lawfulness of –

        (i) an enactment; or

        (ii) a decision, action or failure to act in relation to the exercise of a public function.

    (b) revoked

    (c) revoked

    (d) revoked

    (e) 'the judicial review procedure' means the Part 8 procedure as modified by this Section;

    (f) 'interested party' means any person (other than the claimant and defendant) who is directly affected by the claim; and

    (g) 'court' means the High Court, unless otherwise stated.

(Rule 8.1(6)(b) provides that a rule or practice direction may, in relation to a specified type of proceedings, disapply or modify any of the rules set out in Part 8 as they apply to those proceedings)

Who may exercise the powers of the High Court

54.1A (1) A court officer assigned to the Administrative Court office who is –

    (a) a barrister; or

    (b) a solicitor,

    may exercise the jurisdiction of the High Court with regard to the matters set out in paragraph (2) with the consent of the President of the Queen's Bench Division.

(2) The matters referred to in paragraph (1) are –

    (a) any matter incidental to any proceedings in the High Court;

    (b) any other matter where there is no substantial dispute between the parties; and

    (c) the dismissal of an appeal or application where a party has failed to comply with any order, rule or practice direction.

(3) A court officer may not decide an application for –
- (a) permission to bring judicial review proceedings;
- (b) an injunction;
- (c) a stay of any proceedings, other than a temporary stay of any order or decision of the lower court over a period when the High Court is not sitting or cannot conveniently be convened, unless the parties seek a stay by consent.

(4) Decisions of a court officer may be made without a hearing.

(5) A party may request any decision of a court officer to be reviewed by a judge of the High Court.

(6) At the request of a party, a hearing will be held to reconsider a decision of a court officer, made without a hearing.

(7) A request under paragraph (5) or (6) must be filed within 7 days after the party is served with notice of the decision.

When this Section must be used

54.2 The judicial review procedure must be used in a claim for judicial review where the claimant is seeking –
- (a) a mandatory order;
- (b) a prohibiting order;
- (c) a quashing order; or
- (d) an injunction under section 30 of the Supreme Court Act 1981[1] (restraining a person from acting in any office in which he is not entitled to act).

When this Section may be used

54.3 (1) The judicial review procedure may be used in a claim for judicial review where the claimant is seeking –
- (a) a declaration; or
- (b) an injunction.

(Section 31(2) of the Supreme Court Act 1981 sets out the circumstances in which the court may grant a declaration or injunction in a claim for judicial review)

(Where the claimant is seeking a declaration or injunction in addition to one of the remedies listed in rule 54.2, the judicial review procedure must be used)

(2) A claim for judicial review may include a claim for damages, restitution or the recovery of a sum due but may not seek such a remedy alone.

(Section 31(4) of the Supreme Court Act sets out the circumstances in which the court may award damages, restitution or the recovery of a sum due on a claim for judicial review)

---

[1] 1981 c.54.

Permission required

54.4 The court's permission to proceed is required in a claim for judicial review whether started under this Section or transferred to the Administrative Court.

Time limit for filing claim form

54.5 (A1) In this rule —

'the planning acts' has the same meaning as in section 336 of the Town and Country Planning Act 1990[2];

'decision governed by the Public Contracts Regulations 2006[3]' means any decision the legality of which is or may be affected by a duty owed to an economic operator by virtue of regulation 47A of those Regulations (and for this purpose it does not matter that the claimant is not an economic operator); and

'economic operator' has the same meaning as in regulation 4 of the Public Contracts Regulations 2006.

(1) The claim form must be filed –
  (a) promptly; and
  (b) in any event not later than 3 months after the grounds to make the claim first arose.

(2) The time limits in this rule may not be extended by agreement between the parties.

(3) This rule does not apply when any other enactment specifies a shorter time limit for making the claim for judicial review.

(4) Paragraph (1) does not apply in the cases specified in paragraphs (5) and (6).

(5) Where the application for judicial review relates to a decision made by the Secretary of State or local planning authority under the planning acts, the claim form must be filed not later than six weeks after the grounds to make the claim first arose.

(6) Where the application for judicial review relates to a decision governed by the Public Contracts Regulations 2006, the claim form must be filed within the time within which an economic operator would have been required by regulation 47D(2) of those Regulations (and disregarding the rest of that regulation) to start any proceedings under those Regulations in respect of that decision.

Claim form

54.6 (1) In addition to the matters set out in rule 8.2 (contents of the claim form) the claimant must also state –

---

[2] 1990 c. 8.
[3] S.I. 2006/5, as amended in particular by S.I. 2009/2992 and S.I. 2011/2053.

(a) the name and address of any person he considers to be an interested party;

(b) that he is requesting permission to proceed with a claim for judicial review; and

(c) any remedy (including any interim remedy) he is claiming; and

(d) where appropriate, the grounds on which it is contended that the claim is an Aarhus Convention claim.

(Rules 45.41 to 45.44 make provision about costs in Aarhus Convention claims.)

(Part 25 sets out how to apply for an interim remedy)

(2) The claim form must be accompanied by the documents required by Practice Direction 54A.

Service of claim form

54.7 The claim form must be served on –

(a) the defendant; and

(b) unless the court otherwise directs, any person the claimant considers to be an interested party,

within 7 days after the date of issue.

Judicial review of decisions of the Upper Tribunal

54.7A (1) This rule applies where an application is made, following refusal by the Upper Tribunal of permission to appeal against a decision of the First Tier Tribunal, for judicial review –

(a) of the decision of the Upper Tribunal refusing permission to appeal; or

(b) which relates to the decision of the First Tier Tribunal which was the subject of the application for permission to appeal.

(2) Where this rule applies –

(a) the application may not include any other claim, whether against the Upper Tribunal or not; and

(b) any such other claim must be the subject of a separate application.

(3) The claim form and the supporting documents required by paragraph (4) must be filed no later than 16 days after the date on which notice of the Upper Tribunal's decision was sent to the applicant.

(4) The supporting documents are –

(a) the decision of the Upper Tribunal to which the application relates, and any document giving reasons for the decision;

(b) the grounds of appeal to the Upper Tribunal and any documents which were sent with them;

(c) the decision of the First Tier Tribunal, the application to that Tribunal for permission to appeal and its reasons for refusing permission; and

(d) any other documents essential to the claim.

(5) The claim form and supporting documents must be served on the Upper Tribunal and any other interested party no later than 7 days after the date of issue.

(6) The Upper Tribunal and any person served with the claim form who wishes to take part in the proceedings for judicial review must, no later than 21 days after service of the claim form, file and serve on the applicant and any other party an acknowledgment of service in the relevant practice form.

(7) The court will give permission to proceed only if it considers –

   (a) that there is an arguable case, which has a reasonable prospect of success, that both the decision of the Upper Tribunal refusing permission to appeal and the decision of the First Tier Tribunal against which permission to appeal was sought are wrong in law; and

   (b) that either –

       (i) the claim raises an important point of principle or practice; or

       (ii) there is some other compelling reason to hear it.

(8) If the application for permission is refused on paper without an oral hearing, rule 54.12(3) (request for reconsideration at a hearing) does not apply.

(9) If permission to apply for judicial review is granted –

   (a) if the Upper Tribunal or any interested party wishes there to be a hearing of the substantive application, it must make its request for such a hearing no later than 14 days after service of the order granting permission; and

   (b) if no request for a hearing is made within that period, the court will make a final order quashing the refusal of permission without a further hearing.

(10) The power to make a final order under paragraph (9)(b) may be exercised by the Master of the Crown Office or a Master of the Administrative Court.

Acknowledgment of service

54.8 (1) Any person served with the claim form who wishes to take part in the judicial review must file an acknowledgment of service in the relevant practice form in accordance with the following provisions of this rule.

(2) Any acknowledgment of service must be –

   (a) filed not more than 21 days after service of the claim form; and

   (b) served on –

       (i) the claimant; and

       (ii) subject to any direction under rule 54.7(b), any other person named in the claim form,

   as soon as practicable and, in any event, not later than 7 days after it is filed.

169

(3) The time limits under this rule may not be extended by agreement between the parties.

(4) The acknowledgment of service –

  (a) must –

    (i) where the person filing it intends to contest the claim, set out a summary of his grounds for doing so; and

    (ii) state the name and address of any person the person filing it considers to be an interested party; and

  (b) may include or be accompanied by an application for directions.

(5) Rule 10.3(2) does not apply.

Failure to file acknowledgment of service

54.9 (1) Where a person served with the claim form has failed to file an acknowledgment of service in accordance with rule 54.8, he –

  (a) may not take part in a hearing to decide whether permission should be given unless the court allows him to do so; but

  (b) provided he complies with rule 54.14 or any other direction of the court regarding the filing and service of –

    (i) detailed grounds for contesting the claim or supporting it on additional grounds; and

    (ii) any written evidence,

  may take part in the hearing of the judicial review.

(2) Where that person takes part in the hearing of the judicial review, the court may take his failure to file an acknowledgment of service into account when deciding what order to make about costs.

(3) Rule 8.4 does not apply.

Permission given

54.10 (1) Where permission to proceed is given the court may also give directions.

(2) Directions under paragraph (1) may include –

  (a) a stay of proceedings to which the claim relates;

  (b) directions requiring the proceedings to be heard by a Divisional Court.

Service of order giving or refusing permission

54.11 The court will serve –

  (a) the order giving or refusing permission; and

  (b) any directions,

  on –

    (i) the claimant;

    (ii) the defendant; and

    (iii) any other person who filed an acknowledgment of service.

Permission decision without a hearing

54.12 (1) This rule applies where the court, without a hearing –
    (a)   refuses permission to proceed; or
    (b)   gives permission to proceed –
        (i)   subject to conditions; or
        (ii)   on certain grounds only.

(2)   The court will serve its reasons for making the decision when it serves the order giving or refusing permission in accordance with rule 54.11.

(3)   Subject to paragraph (7), the claimant may not appeal but may request the decision to be reconsidered at a hearing.

(4)   A request under paragraph (3) must be filed within 7 days after service of the reasons under paragraph (2).

(5)   The claimant, defendant and any other person who has filed an acknowledgment of service will be given at least 2 days' notice of the hearing date.

(6)   The court may give directions requiring the proceedings to be heard by a Divisional Court.

(7)   Where the court refuses permission to proceed and records the fact that the application is totally without merit in accordance with rule 23.12, the claimant may not request that decision to be reconsidered at a hearing.

Defendant etc. may not apply to set aside

54.13 Neither the defendant nor any other person served with the claim form may apply to set aside an order giving permission to proceed.

Response

54.14 (1) A defendant and any other person served with the claim form who wishes to contest the claim or support it on additional grounds must file and serve –
    (a)   detailed grounds for contesting the claim or supporting it on additional grounds; and
    (b)   any written evidence,
within 35 days after service of the order giving permission.

(2)   The following rules do not apply –
    (a)   rule 8.5 (3) and 8.5 (4)(defendant to file and serve written evidence at the same time as acknowledgment of service); and
    (b)   rule 8.5 (5) and 8.5(6) (claimant to file and serve any reply within 14 days).

Where claimant seeks to rely on additional grounds

54.15 The court's permission is required if a claimant seeks to rely on grounds other than those for which he has been given permission to proceed.

Evidence

54.16 (1) Rule 8.6 (1) does not apply.

(2) No written evidence may be relied on unless –

    (a) it has been served in accordance with any –

        (i) rule under this Section; or

        (ii) direction of the court; or

    (b) the court gives permission.

Court's powers to hear any person

54.17 (1) Any person may apply for permission –

    (a) to file evidence; or

    (b) make representations at the hearing of the judicial review.

(2) An application under paragraph (1) should be made promptly.

Judicial review may be decided without a hearing

54.18 The court may decide the claim for judicial review without a hearing where all the parties agree.

Court's powers in respect of quashing orders

54.19 (1) This rule applies where the court makes a quashing order in respect of the decision to which the claim relates.

(2) The court may –

    (a)

        (i) remit the matter to the decision-maker; and

        (ii) direct it to reconsider the matter and reach a decision in accordance with the judgment of the court; or

    (b) in so far as any enactment permits, substitute its own decision for the decision to which the claim relates.

(Section 31 of the Supreme Court Act 1981[4] enables the High Court, subject to certain conditions, to substitute its own decision for the decision in question.)

Transfer

54.20 The court may

    (a) order a claim to continue as if it had not been started under this Section; and

    (b) where it does so, give directions about the future management of the claim.

(Part 30 (transfer) applies to transfers to and from the Administrative Court)

---

[4] 1981 c.54. Section 31 is amended by section 141 of the Tribunals, Courts and Enforcement Act 2007 (c. 15).

II PLANNING COURT

General
54.21 (1) This Section applies to Planning Court claims.
(2) In this Section, 'Planning Court claim' means a judicial review or statutory challenge which —
    (a) involves any of the following matters —
        (i) planning permission, other development consents, the enforcement of planning control and the enforcement of other statutory schemes;
        (ii) applications under the Transport and Works Act 1992;
        (iii) wayleaves;
        (iv) highways and other rights of way;
        (v) compulsory purchase orders;
        (vi) village greens;
        (vii) European Union environmental legislation and domestic transpositions, including assessments for development consents, habitats, waste and pollution control;
        (viii) national, regional or other planning policy documents, statutory or otherwise; or
        (ix) any other matter the judge appointed under rule 54.22(2) considers appropriate; and
    (b) has been issued or transferred to the Planning Court.
    (Part 30 (Transfer) applies to transfers to and from the Planning Court.)

Specialist list
54.22 (1) The Planning Court claims form a specialist list.
(2) A judge nominated by the President of the Queen's Bench Division will be in charge of the Planning Court specialist list and will be known as the Planning Liaison Judge.
(3) The President of the Queen's Bench Division will be responsible for the nomination of specialist planning judges to deal with Planning Court claims which are significant within the meaning of Practice Direction 54E, and of other judges to deal with other Planning Court claims.

Application of the Civil Procedure Rules
54.23 These Rules and their practice directions will apply to Planning Court claims unless this section or a practice direction provides otherwise.

Further provision about Planning Court claims
54.24 Practice Direction 54E makes further provision about Planning Court claims, in particular about the timescales for determining such claims.

APPENDIX HA

[Insert Civil Procedure Rules: Practice Direction 54E – Planning Court Claims]

PRACTICE DIRECTION 54E – PLANNING COURT CLAIMS
This Practice Direction supplements Part 54

General

1.1 This Practice Direction applies to Planning Court claims.

How to start a Planning Court claim

2.1 Planning Court claims must be issued or lodged in the Administrative Court Office of the High Court in accordance with Practice Direction 54D.

2.2 The form must be marked the 'Planning Court'.

Categorisation of Planning Court claims

3.1 Planning Court claims may be categorised as 'significant' by the Planning Liaison Judge.

3.2 Significant Planning Court claims include claims which—

a)   relate to commercial, residential, or other developments which have significant economic impact either at a local level or beyond their immediate locality;

b)   raise important points of law;

c)   generate significant public interest; or

d)   by virtue of the volume or nature of technical material, are best dealt with by judges with significant experience of handling such matters.

3.3 A party wishing to make representations in respect of the categorisation of a Planning Court claim must do so in writing, on issuing the claim or lodging an acknowledgment of service as appropriate.

3.4 The target timescales for the hearing of significant (as defined by paragraph 3.2) Planning Court claims, which the parties should prepare to meet, are as follows, subject to the overriding objective of the interests of justice—

a)   applications for permission to apply for judicial review are to be determined within three weeks of the expiry of the time limit for filing of the acknowledgment of service;

b)   oral renewals of applications for permission to apply for judicial review are to be heard within one month of receipt of request for renewal;

c) applications for permission under section 289 of the Town and Country Planning Act 1990 are to be determined within one month of issue;

d) substantive statutory applications, including applications under section 288 of the Town and Country Planning Act 1990, are to be heard within six months of issue; and

e) judicial reviews are to be heard within ten weeks of the expiry of the period for the submission of detailed grounds by the defendant or any other party as provided in Rule 54.14.

3.5 The Planning Court may make case management directions, including a direction to any party intending to contest the claim to file and serve a summary of his grounds for doing so.

3.6 Notwithstanding the categorisation under paragraph 3.1 of a Planning Court claim as significant or otherwise, the Planning Liaison Judge may direct the expedition of any Planning Court claim if he considers it to necessary to deal with the case justly.

APPENDIX I

[Insert New version of Pre-action Protocol for Judicial Review]

Pre-Action Protocol for Judicial Review

INTRODUCTION
This protocol applies to proceedings within England and Wales only. It does not affect the time limit specified by Rule 54.5(1) of the Civil Procedure Rules which requires that any claim form in an application for judicial review must be filed promptly and in any event not later than 3 months after the grounds to make the claim first arose or the shorter time limits specified by Rules 54.5(5) and (6) which set out that a claim form for certain planning judicial reviews must be filed within 6 weeks and the claim form for certain procurement judicial reviews must be filed within 30 days.[1]

1 Judicial review allows people with a sufficient interest in a decision or action by a public body to ask a judge to review the lawfulness of:
   * an enactment; or
   * a decision, action or failure to act in relation to the exercise of a public function.[2]
2 Judicial review may be used where there is no right of appeal or where all avenues of appeal have been exhausted.

Alternative Dispute Resolution
3.1 The parties should consider whether some form of alternative dispute resolution procedure would be more suitable than litigation, and if so, endeavour to agree which form to adopt. Both the Claimant and Defendant may be required by the Court to provide evidence that alternative means of resolving their dispute were considered. The Courts take the view that litigation should be a last resort, and that claims should not be issued prematurely when a settlement is still actively being explored. Parties are warned that if the protocol is not followed (including this paragraph) then the Court must have regard to such conduct when determining costs. However, parties should also note that a claim for judicial review 'must be filed promptly and in any event not later than 3 months after the grounds to make the claim first arose'.

---

[1] While the court does have the discretion under Rule 3.1(2)(a) of the Civil Procedure Rules to allow a late claim, this is only used in exceptional circumstances. **Compliance with the protocol alone is unlikely to be sufficient to persuade the court to allow a late claim.**
[2] Civil Procedure Rule 54.1(2).

3.2 It is not practicable in this protocol to address in detail how the parties might decide which method to adopt to resolve their particular dispute. However, summarised below are some of the options for resolving disputes without litigation:

- Discussion and negotiation.
- Ombudsmen – the Parliamentary and Health Service and the Local Government Ombudsmen have discretion to deal with complaints relating to maladministration. The British and Irish Ombudsman Association provide information about Ombudsman schemes and other complaint handling bodies and this is available from their website at www.bioa.org.uk. Parties may wish to note that the Ombudsmen are not able to look into a complaint once court action has been commenced.
- Early neutral evaluation by an independent third party (for example, a lawyer experienced in the field of administrative law or an individual experienced in the subject matter of the claim).
- Mediation – a form of facilitated negotiation assisted by an independent neutral party.

3.3 The Legal Services Commission has published a booklet on 'Alternatives to Court', CLS Direct Information Leaflet 23 (www.clsdirect.org.uk), which lists a number of organisations that provide alternative dispute resolution services.

3.4 It is expressly recognised that no party can or should be forced to mediate or enter into any form of ADR.

4 **Judicial review may not be appropriate in every instance.**

Claimants are strongly advised to seek appropriate legal advice when considering such proceedings and, in particular, before adopting this protocol or making a claim. Although the Legal Services Commission will not normally grant full representation before a letter before claim has been sent and the proposed defendant given a reasonable time to respond, initial funding may be available, for eligible claimants, to cover the work necessary to write this. (See Annex C for more information.)

5 This protocol sets out a code of good practice and contains the steps which parties should generally follow before making a claim for judicial review.

6 This protocol does not impose a greater obligation on a public body to disclose documents or give reasons for its decision than that already provided for in statute or common law. However, where the court considers that a public body should have provided relevant documents and/or information, particularly where this failure is a breach of a statutory or common law requirement, it may impose sanctions.

This protocol will not be appropriate where the defendant does not have the legal power to change the decision being challenged, for example decisions issued by tribunals such as the Asylum and Immigration Tribunal.

This protocol will not be appropriate in urgent cases, for example, when directions have been set, or are in force, for the claimant's removal from the UK, or where there is an urgent need for an interim order to compel a public body to act where it has unlawfully refused to do so (for example, the failure of a local housing authority to secure interim accommodation for a homeless claimant) a claim should be made immediately. A letter before claim will not stop the implementation of a disputed decision in all instances.

This protocol may not be appropriate in cases where one of the shorter time limits in Rules 54.5(5) or (6) applies. In those cases, the parties should still attempt to comply with this protocol but the court will not apply normal cost sanctions where the court is satisfied that it has not been possible to comply because of the shorter time limits.

7   All claimants will need to satisfy themselves whether they should follow the protocol, depending upon the circumstances of his or her case. Where the use of the protocol is appropriate, the court will normally expect all parties to have complied with it and will take into account compliance or non-compliance when giving directions for case management of proceedings or when making orders for costs.[3] However, even in emergency cases, it is good practice to fax to the defendant the draft Claim Form which the claimant intends to issue. A claimant is also normally required to notify a defendant when an interim mandatory order is being sought.

The letter before claim

8   Before making a claim, the claimant should send a letter to the defendant. The purpose of this letter is to identify the issues in dispute and establish whether litigation can be avoided.

9   Claimants should normally use the suggested **standard format** for the letter outlined at Annex A.

10   The letter should contain **the date and details of the decision, act or omission being challenged and a clear summary of the facts** on which the claim is based. It should also contain the **details of any relevant information** that the claimant is seeking and an explanation of why this is considered relevant. If the claim is considered to be an Aarhus Convention claim, the letter should state this clearly and explain the reasons, since specific rules as to costs apply to such claims.

11   The letter should normally contain the **details of any interested parties**[4] known to the claimant. They should be sent a copy of the letter before

---

[3] Civil Procedure Rules Costs Practice Direction.
[4] See Civil Procedure Rule 54.1(2)(f).

claim for information. **Claimants are** strongly advised to seek appropriate legal advice **when considering such proceedings and, in particular, before sending the letter before claim to other interested parties or making a claim.**

12   A claim should not normally be made until the proposed reply date given in the letter before claim has passed, unless the circumstances of the case require more immediate action to be taken.

The letter of response

13   Defendants should normally respond within 14 days using the **standard format** at Annex B. Failure to do so will be taken into account by the court and sanctions may be imposed unless there are good reasons.[5]

14   Where it is not possible to reply within the proposed time limit the defendant should send an interim reply and propose a reasonable extension. Where an extension is sought, reasons should be given and, where required, additional information requested. This will not affect the time limit for making a claim for judicial review [6]nor will it bind the claimant where he or she considers this to be unreasonable. However, where the court considers that a subsequent claim is made prematurely it may impose sanctions.

15   If the **claim is being conceded in full,** the reply should say so in clear and unambiguous terms.

16   If the **claim is being conceded in part or not being conceded at all,** the reply should say so in clear and unambiguous terms, and:

    (a)   where appropriate, contain a new decision, clearly identifying what aspects of the claim are being conceded and what are not, or, give a clear timescale within which the new decision will be issued;

    (b)   provide a fuller explanation for the decision, if considered appropriate to do so;

    (c)   address any points of dispute, or explain why they cannot be addressed;

    (d)   enclose any **relevant** documentation requested by the claimant, or explain why the documents are not being enclosed; and

    (e)   where appropriate, confirm whether or not they will oppose any application for an interim remedy.

If the letter before claim has stated that the claim is an Aarhus Convention claim but the defendant does not accept this, the reply should state this clearly and explain the reasons.

---

[5] See Civil Procedure Rules Pre-action Protocol Practice Direction paragraphs 2–3.
[6] See Civil Procedure Rule 54.5(1).

17   The response should be sent to **all interested parties**[7] identified by the claimant and contain details of any other parties who the defendant considers also have an interest.

A LETTER BEFORE CLAIM

SECTION 1. INFORMATION REQUIRED IN A LETTER BEFORE CLAIM
Proposed claim for judicial review

1 To
(Insert the name and address of the proposed defendant – see details in section 2)

2 The claimant
(Insert the title, first and last name and the address of the claimant)

3 Reference details
(When dealing with large organisations it is important to understand that the information relating to any particular individual's previous dealings with it may not be immediately available, therefore it is important to set out the relevant reference numbers for the matter in dispute and/or the identity of those within the public body who have been handling the particular matter in dispute – see details in section 3)

4 The details of the matter being challenged
(Set out clearly the matter being challenged, particularly if there has been more than one decision)

5 The issue
(Set out the date and details of the decision, or act or omission being challenged, a brief summary of the facts and why it is contented to be wrong)

6 The details of the action that the defendant is expected to take
(Set out the details of the remedy sought, including whether a review or any interim remedy are being requested)

7 The details of the legal advisers, if any, dealing with this claim
(Set out the name, address and reference details of any legal advisers dealing with the claim)

---

[7] See Civil Procedure Rule 54.1(2)(f).

8 The details of any interested parties

(Set out the details of any interested parties and confirm that they have been sent a copy of this letter)

9 The details of any information sought

(Set out the details of any information that is sought. This may include a request for a fuller explanation of the reasons for the decision that is being challenged)

10 The details of any documents that are considered relevant and necessary

(Set out the details of any documentation or policy in respect of which the disclosure is sought and explain why these are relevant. If you rely on a statutory duty to disclose, this should be specified)

11 The address for reply and service of court documents

(Insert the address for the reply)

12 Proposed reply date

(The precise time will depend upon the circumstances of the individual case. However, although a shorter or longer time may be appropriate in a particular case, 14 days is a reasonable time to allow in most circumstances)

SECTION 2. ADDRESS FOR SENDING THE LETTER BEFORE CLAIM

Public bodies have requested that, for certain types of cases, in order to ensure a prompt response, letters before claim should be sent to specific addresses.

- **Where the claim concerns a decision in an Immigration, Asylum or Nationality case:**
  - The claim may be sent electronically to the following email address UKVIPAP@homeoffice.gsi.gov.uk
  - Alternatively the claim may be sent by post to the following UK Border Agency postal address:

  Judicial Review Unit
  UK Border Agency
  Lunar House
  40 Awellesley Rd
  Croydon CR9 2BY
- **Where the claim concerns a decision by the Legal Services Commission:**
  - The address on the decision letter/notification;

  Legal Director
  Corporate Legal Team

Legal Services Commission
102 Petty France
London SW1H 9AJ

- **Where the claim concerns a decision by a local authority:**
  - — The address on the decision letter/notification; and
  - — Their legal department[8]
- **Where the claim concerns a decision by a department or body for whom Treasury Solicitor acts** and Treasury Solicitor has already been involved in the case **a copy should also be sent, quoting the Treasury Solicitor's reference,** to:

The Treasury Solicitor,
One Kemble Street,
London WC2B 4TS

In all other circumstances, the letter should be sent to the address on the letter notifying the decision.

SECTION 3. SPECIFIC REFERENCE DETAILS REQUIRED
Public bodies have requested that the following information should be provided in order to ensure prompt response.

- **Where the claim concerns an Immigration, Asylum or Nationality case, dependent upon the nature of the case:**
  - — The Home Office reference number
  - — The Port reference number
  - — The Asylum and Immigration Tribunal reference number
  - — The National Asylum Support Service reference number
  Or, if these are unavailable:
  - — The full name, nationality and date of birth of the claimant.
- **Where the claim concerns a decision by the Legal Services Commission:**
  - — The certificate reference number.

B RESPONSE TO A LETTER BEFORE CLAIM

INFORMATION REQUIRED IN A RESPONSE TO A LETTER BEFORE CLAIM
Proposed claim for judicial review

1 The claimant
(Insert the title, first and last names and the address to which any reply should be sent)

---

[8] The relevant address should be available from a range of sources such as the Phone Book; Business and Services Directory, Thomson's Local Directory, CAB, etc.

2 From
(Insert the name and address of the defendant)

3 Reference details
(Set out the relevant reference numbers for the matter in dispute and the identity of those within the public body who have been handling the issue)

4 The details of the matter being challenged
(Set out details of the matter being challenged, providing a fuller explanation of the decision, where this is considered appropriate)

5 Response to the proposed claim
(Set out whether the issue in question is conceded in part, or in full, or will be contested. Where it is not proposed to disclose any information that has been requested, explain the reason for this. Where an interim reply is being sent and there is a realistic prospect of settlement, details should be included)

6 Details of any other interested parties
(Identify any other parties who you consider have an interest who have not already been sent a letter by the claimant)

7 Address for further correspondence and service of court documents
(Set out the address for any future correspondence on this matter)

C NOTES ON PUBLIC FUNDING FOR LEGAL COSTS IN JUDICIAL REVIEW
Public funding for legal costs in judicial review is available from legal professionals and advice agencies which have contracts with the Legal Services Commission as part of the Community Legal Service. Funding may be provided for:

- Legal Help to provide initial advice and assistance with any legal problem; or
- Legal Representation to allow you to be represented in court if you are taking or defending court proceedings. This is available in two forms:
  - Investigative Help is limited to funding to investigate the strength of the proposed claim. It includes the issue and conduct of proceedings only so far as is necessary to obtain disclosure of relevant information or to protect the client's position in relation to any urgent hearing or time limit for the issue of proceedings. This includes the work necessary to write a letter before claim to the body potentially under challenge, setting out the grounds of challenge, and giving

that body a reasonable opportunity, typically 14 days, in which to respond.

— Full Representation is provided to represent you in legal proceedings and includes litigation services, advocacy services, and all such help as is usually given by a person providing representation in proceedings, including steps preliminary or incidental to proceedings, and/or arriving at or giving effect to a compromise to avoid or bring to an end any proceedings. Except in emergency cases, a proper letter before claim must be sent and the other side must be given an opportunity to respond before Full Representation is granted.

Further information on the type(s) of help available and the criteria for receiving that help may be found in the Legal Service Manual Volume 3: "The Funding Code". This may be found on the Legal Services Commission website at:

www.legalservices.gov.uk

A list of contracted firms and Advice Agencies may be found on the Community Legal Services website at:

www.justask.org.uk

APPENDIX L

N463 Application for Urgent Consideration

[Insert new version of N463 Application for Urgent Consideration]

The form reproduced overleaf is available to download from *http://hmcts-courtfinder.justice.gov.uk/courtfinder/forms/n463-eng.pdf.*

Judicial Review
Application for urgent consideration

Click here to reset form	Click here to print form

In the High Court of Justice
Administrative Court

This form must be completed by the Claimant or the Claimant's advocate if exceptional urgency is being claimed and the application needs to be determined within a certain time scale.

The claimant, or the claimant's solicitors must serve this form on the defendant(s) and any interested parties with the N461 Judicial review claim form.

To the Defendant(s) and Interested Party(ies)
Representations as to the urgency of the claim may be made by defendants or interested parties to the relevant Administrative Court Office by fax or email:-

For cases proceeding in

Claim No.	
Claimant(s) *(including ref.)*	
Defendant(s)	
Interested Party(ies)	

London	
Fax: 020 7947 6802	**email:** administrativecourtoffice.generaloffice@hmcts.x.gsi.gov.uk
Birmingham	
Fax: 0121 250 6730	**email:** administrativecourtoffice.birmingham@hmcts.x.gsi.gov.uk
Cardiff	
Fax: 02920 376461	**email:** administrativecourtoffice.cardiff@hmcts.x.gsi.gov.uk
Leeds	
Fax: 0113 306 2581	**email:** administrativecourtoffice.leeds@hmcts.x.gsi.gov.uk
Manchester	
Fax: 0161 240 5315	**email:** administrativecourtoffice.manchester@hmcts.x.gsi.gov.uk

SECTION 1 Reasons for urgency

SECTION 2 Proposed timetable *(tick the boxes and complete the following statements that apply)*

☐ a) The N461 application for permission should be considered within _____ hours/days

   If consideration is sought within 48 hours, you must complete Section 3 below

☐ b) Abridgement of time is sought for the lodging of acknowledgments of service

☐ c) If permission for judicial review is granted, a substantive hearing is sought by _____ (date)

SECTION 3 Justification for request for immediate consideration

If it is decided that your application will be dealt with as an immediate application, we will notify you of the outcome by email as soon as the judge has reached a determination. You will subsequently be sent a hard copy of the judges order in the post. Please provide an email address to which you would like notification sent.

Email address:

Please note: if you do not provide a valid email address, you will only be notified of the outcome by post, which will take at least 2 – 3 days to be processed and delivered.

Date and time when it was first appreciated that an immediate application might be necessary.

Date

Time

Please provide reasons for any delay in making the application.

What efforts have been made to put the defendant and any interested party on notice of the application?

SECTION 4 Interim relief *(state what interim relief is sought and why in the box below)*
A draft order must be attached.

SECTION 5 Service

A copy of this form of application was served on the defendant(s) and interested parties as follows:

Defendant

☐ by fax machine to   time sent
  Fax no.   time

☐ by handing it to or leaving it with
  name

☐ by e-mail to
  e-mail address

Date served
  Date

Interested party

☐ by fax machine to   time sent
  Fax no.   time

☐ by handing it to or leaving it with
  name

☐ by e-mail to
  e-mail address

Date served
  Date

I confirm that all relevant facts have been disclosed in this application

Name of claimant's advocate
  name

Claimant (claimant's advocate)
  Signed

Index

191